The Repugnant Conclusion

The Repugnant Conclusion is a controversial theorem about population size. It states that a sufficiently large population of lives that are barely worth living is better than a smaller population of high-quality lives. This is highly counter-intuitive. It implies that we can improve the world by trading quality of life for quantity of lives. Can it be defended?

Christopher Cowie explores these questions and unpacks the controversies surrounding the Repugnant Conclusion. He focuses on whether the truth of the Repugnant Conclusion turns – as some have claimed – on the uncomfortable claim that many people's lives are actually *bad* for them and that even privileged people lead lives that are only just worth living.

Highly recommended for those interested in ethics, applied ethics and population studies *The Repugnant Conclusion* will also be of interest to those in related disciplines such as economics, development studies, politics and international relations.

Christopher Cowie is Assistant Professor in Philosophy at the University of Durham, UK. He is the author of *Morality and Epistemic Judgment*: *The Argument from Analogy* (2019), and co-editor of *Companions in Guilt Arguments in Metaethics*, also published by Routledge.

Routledge Focus on Philosophy

Routledge Focus on Philosophy is an exciting and innovative new series, capturing and disseminating some of the best and most exciting new research in philosophy in short book form. Peer reviewed and at a maximum of fifty thousand words shorter than the typical research monograph, *Routledge Focus on Philosophy* titles are available in both ebook and print on demand format. Tackling big topics in a digestible format the series opens up important philosophical research for a wider audience, and as such is invaluable reading for the scholar, researcher and student seeking to keep their finger on the pulse of the discipline. The series also reflects the growing interdisciplinarity within philosophy and will be of interest to those in related disciplines across the humanities and social sciences.

Extended Consciousness and Predictive Processing
A Third Wave View
Michael D. Kirchhoff and Julian Kiverstein

What We Ought and What We Can
Alex King

The Ethics of Whistleblowing
Eric R. Boot

Totalitarianism and Philosophy
Alan Haworth

The Repugnant Conclusion
A Philosophical Inquiry
Christopher Cowie

For more information about this series, please visit: www.routledge.com/Routledge-Focus-on-Philosophy/book-series/RFP

The Repugnant Conclusion

A Philosophical Inquiry

Christopher Cowie

LONDON AND NEW YORK

First published 2020
by Routledge
4 Park Square, Milton Park, Abingdon, Oxon OX14 4RN
605 Third Avenue, New York, NY 10017

First issued in paperback 2023

Routledge is an imprint of the Taylor & Francis Group, an informa business

British Library Cataloguing-in-Publication Data
A catalogue record for this book is available from the British Library

Library of Congress Cataloging-in-Publication Data
A catalog record has been requested for this book

ISBN: 978-1-03-257045-7 (pbk)
ISBN: 978-1-138-60544-2 (hbk)
ISBN: 978-0-429-46811-7 (ebk)

DOI: 10.4324/9780429468117

Typeset in Times New Roman
by Deanta Global Publishing Services, Chennai, India

Publisher's Note
The publisher has gone to great lengths to ensure the quality of this reprint but
points out that some imperfections in the original copies may be apparent.

For Rugby Street, Belfast.
High Average Welfare, Low Population.

Contents

Acknowledgements

I am grateful to everyone who has read and commented on earlier drafts of this manuscript – especially Torbjorn Tännsjö, Clark Wolf, Guy Fletcher, Anneli Jefferson, Thomas Petersen, Roderick Cowie and an anonymous referee for Routledge – and to audiences in Cambridge, Edinburgh, Santa Fe, London, Glasgow, Sheffield and Cumberland Lodge. Thanks also to my students at Durham – Tom Chapman, Helena Pilcher, Anya Southby and Tom Pymer – for engaging with this material during its writing.

I am especially grateful to Partha Dasgupta for guiding me through this material and to Tim Crane for providing the opportunity.

1   Introduction

The Repugnant Conclusion is a controversial theorem about population size. It states that enormous populations of lives that are barely worth living can be – and sometimes are – better than small populations of high-quality lives. This is highly counter-intuitive. Hence, the controversial nature of the theorem. The aim of this book is to explore whether, despite this, it might nonetheless be true. More specifically, the aim is to explore a particularly striking defence of its truth. This defence is based on an uncomfortable claim about the quality of our lives. It is that many people's lives are actually *bad* for them and even privileged people lead lives that are only just worth living. The thought is that if *this* is true, then the Repugnant Conclusion is true too.

There is a lot going on here. We need to put some foundations in place. The best place to start is with the idea that we can *evaluate* different populations. It is the most fundamental assumption behind all of our subsequent reasoning and argumentation. Strange though it may sound, it is something that we are all familiar with. An ordinary example illustrates. In 1800, the world's population was close to one billion. It is now closer to eight billion and growing.[1] It is projected to continue to grow well into this century. This is one of the most serious challenges of our time. In his classic book, *The Population Bomb*, Paul Ehrlich gave clear voice to it:

> Too many cars, too many factories, too much detergent, too many pesticides, multiplying contrails, inadequate sewage treatment plants, too little water, too much carbon dioxide – all can be traced easily to too many people.
>
> Ehrlich 1968: 66

Ehrlich claimed that there were *too many* people ('Too Many People' is the title of part 1 of chapter 1 of his book). He has continued to voice this concern over the decades, since the publication of *The Population Bomb*.

Economists and geographers, social commentators and politicians increasingly follow him in this. Don't worry about the *truth* of Ehrlich's claim; it may or may not be true. Instead, note an assumption that he and others are making. They are assuming that – in at least some cases – we can compare (or evaluate or rank) populations of different sizes. We can establish that some are better or worse than others. Without this assumption, they could not say that some populations are *too big*.

This raises an obvious question. How can we do this? What principles allow us to work out which of two or more different possible populations is better or worse?[2] Sometimes the comparison may seem obvious; given the earth's current resources populations of over fifty billion will obviously be worse than populations of ten billion. Clearly articulating *why* this is the case is more challenging, however, and some comparisons are much less obvious. This is especially true when we are sensitive to the fact that *welfare* or *quality of life* (I use these as synonyms throughout) is likely to vary as population size varies. Suppose, for example, that we compare a population of eight billion people all of whom lead lives of a reasonably high quality with a population of ten million people, all of whom lead lives of a significantly higher quality. Which is better, and why? What about a billion people with a quality of life somewhere between these two extremes? How would this compare? Or suppose that in the near future human population can expand without constraints based on the limited resources of our planet (there are, as economists would say, no 'externalities'). Should we then aim to populate the galaxy? Would a human population of many trillion people, all of whom lead a good quality of life, be any better than the billions that we already have? If not, why not?

Philosophers have been engaged in the search for the general principles that allow us to answer these difficult questions for the past forty years. They have not arrived at any satisfactory answers. On the contrary. Not only have they been unable to find the general principles that they are looking for, they have also generated scepticism about whether any such principles *could* be found. This is, in part at least, because otherwise plausible-seeming principles have a tendency to yield highly counter-intuitive consequences. One of the most troubling – and stubbornest – of all of these counter-intuitive consequences is the Repugnant Conclusion. Although it arguably dates to the great nineteenth century philosopher Henry Sidgwick, this result owes its contemporary prominence to Derek Parfit's compelling presentation in his classic book *Reasons and Persons*. In Part IV of that book, Parfit noted that some very plausible reasoning about what such a principle would look like led to a very *implausible* conclusion indeed. He presented it as follows:

> For any possible population of at least ten billion people, all with a
> very high quality of life, there must be some much larger imaginable

population whose existence, if other things are equal, would be better even though its members have lives that are barely worth living.

Parfit 1984: 388

This is the Repugnant Conclusion. As we will see below, the above quotation isn't actually the best way of articulating it, but the basic idea comes across clearly enough nonetheless. It is that enormous populations in which everyone has a life that is barely worth living can nonetheless be better than small populations in which everyone enjoys a great quality of life. This struck Parfit as clearly false; so much so that he labelled it 'repugnant'. It continues to strike many who encounter it today in just this way. If anything, its counter-intuitiveness probably resonates to an even greater extent today than when Parfit first published it; world population now stands at eight billion and concerns about over-population understandably occupy an increasingly prominent place in the contemporary social consciousness and political agenda – more so than when Ehrlich or Parfit were initially writing. Given this, the fact that, as Parfit demonstrated, very plausible reasoning seems to show that it is true will strike many as strongly counter-intuitive.

One of the aims of this book is to explain the 'very plausible reasoning' that leads to this counter-intuitive conclusion. This is the task of chapter 1. The other aim – the main aim, in fact – is to examine a particularly interesting *defence* of it. That defence is based on the uncomfortable truth that many people's lives are actually *bad* for them and even privileged people lead lives that are only just worth living. I refer to this throughout as the Quality of Life Strategy. This is the title of chapter 2. It may not be obvious how or why this 'uncomfortable truth' could be a defence of the Repugnant Conclusion. To see why it could be, take a step back to think about the *structure* of the problem that we face. It is that extremely plausible reasoning yields an extremely counter-intuitive conclusion. The basic structure is familiar to philosophers as that of a *paradox*. This is a perfectly general structure of problem that appears when we think about fundamentals in many different areas of enquiry: space and time, the composition of matter, the nature of mind, and value (to name a few).[3] It is surprisingly common to find that our most basic beliefs about them yield a wildly implausible result. Whatever the subject-matter, there are two ways of dealing with a paradox. One is to reject the reasoning that leads to the implausible conclusion. This requires identifying where the reasoning goes wrong. The second is to accept the conclusion. This requires explaining why it *seems* wildly counter-intuitive, though in fact it is not. The Quality of Life Strategy is an attempt to defend this second option. It is an attempt to explain why, though the Repugnant Conclusion seems wildly counter-intuitive, it is in fact true.

How could this be? The basic idea is as follows. The Repugnant Conclusion seems false because we imagine lives that are barely worth living as really terrible things. We imagine them as being like the lives of the most terribly unfortunate people; as, for example, lives without meaning or hope, or as lives lived below the poverty line. If that were accurate, then the Repugnant Conclusion really would be unacceptable: an enormous number of lives like these couldn't be better than a small number of great lives. But, according to the Quality of Life Strategy, it is not accurate. When we imagine lives that are barely worth living, we should in fact imagine lives that are much better than this. We should imagine lives like those of fortunate, prosperous people. Lives without meaning or hope, or lives lived below the poverty line are *worse* than this. Now suppose that this is true. The Repugnant Conclusion is no longer obviously false. Its seeming falsity is the result of mis-imagining what a life that is barely worth living is in fact like. It is a result of imagining it to be worse than it in fact is. We have resolved the paradox. We can accept the Repugnant Conclusion and the plausible reasoning that it follows from.

This strategy has been defended by some of the most prominent contributors to the field. My aim is to fairly and fully present and assess it. I set out to *defend* it. In chapters 2 and 3, I show that it is more robust than one might think. It can – if properly understood – be defended against common criticisms. Nevertheless, in chapter 4, I argue that it fails. We cannot resolve the paradox in this way. This is disappointing. As with many purported solutions in the study of population, the real issue is that the Quality of Life Strategy has deeply implausible consequences when we attempt to *generalise* with it; to tease out its consequences in the context of new comparisons of populations. Two of these implausible consequences concern variants on the Repugnant Conclusion: the *Very Repugnant Conclusion* and the *Reverse Repugnant Conclusion*. I explain what these are later. The basic problem though is that the Quality of Life Strategy runs aground on them. This is not, in itself, a novel conclusion. Both the Very Repugnant Conclusion and the Reverse Repugnant Conclusion are familiar in the literature. That they represent a serious challenge to the Quality of Life Strategy is well-known. And whilst ultimately I agree, I make two novel contributions along the way. Firstly, I show that the route from the Very Repugnant Conclusion and the Reverse Repugnant Conclusion to the failure of the Quality of Life Strategy is a long and tortuous one that depends on *how* one reasons to the Repugnant Conclusion (a point that is often missed). Secondly, I show that there are conditions – interestingly similar conditions – under which these serious challenges could be avoided but that these conditions cannot be met. All of this is illustrated at length in chapter 4.

The roadmap is as follows. In chapter 2, I present and contextualise three basic arguments for the Repugnant Conclusion. This includes some background material on the assessment of populations (section 2.2) that, while not strictly necessary, is interesting and important nonetheless. Seasoned 'population ethicists' may wish to skip some of it. In chapter 3, I present, clarify and motivate the Quality of Life Strategy as a means of defending the Repugnant Conclusion. I note that there are in fact a range of different interpretations of it. I articulate the strongest. In chapter 4, I develop two objections to it – one concerning the Very Repugnant Conclusion, the other concerning the Reverse Repugnant Conclusion – and explain how a defender of the Quality of Life Strategy should respond to them. I conclude that this response is not good enough. It goes without saying that there is much ground that I am unable to cover and a great deal more that I cover more quickly than I would like. This is unavoidable. The assessment of populations – even in the highly theoretical sense that I am concerned with – is a very large field and there is a great deal of technical work that I do not touch on here. Nevertheless, my hope is that this short book can be a useful tool both for those who are new to the field or new to moral philosophy (especially chapter 2), as well as for seasoned moral philosophers and population ethicists.

Notes

1 United Nations Population Division. https://population.un.org/wpp/.
2 A further, related question is what principles allow us to work out what the optimal population size is. See e.g. Dasgupta 1969, 2005 and Greaves forthcoming.
3 See e.g. Sainsbury 2009.

2   The Repugnant Conclusion

The Repugnant Conclusion is a controversial theorem that compares the values of different populations. It tells us that:

> For any possible population of at least ten billion people, all with a very high quality of life, there must be some much larger imaginable population whose existence, if other things are equal, would be better even though its members have lives that are barely worth living.

Parfit 1984: 388

There are many ways of getting to this theorem; the Repugnant Conclusion is the result of several quite distinct lines of reasoning. That is perhaps one of the reasons that it is worth taking seriously. Results that can (seemingly) be derived in independent ways are robust. The aim of this chapter is to set these different lines of reasoning out clearly. Having done this, we should have a clear idea of why one might think the Repugnant Conclusion is true. We begin with the simplest line of reasoning. I refer to it as 'totalist reasoning'. This is followed by 'continuum reasoning' and 'dominance addition reasoning' respectively. Each line of reasoning is slightly more complex than its predecessor. Although not everyone would agree, I believe that each is also more plausible than its predecessor.

2.1 Totalist reasoning

The Repugnant Conclusion is a comparative claim about populations. By 'populations' I mean sets of people in which there are two variables: the number of lives within each set, and the quality of each of those lives. So, for example, suppose that we consider two populations, call them X and Y respectively, as represented in the diagram below (Figure 2.1).

  In this diagram – and subsequent diagrams – each rectangle represents a population. The height of a rectangle represents the quality of life of each

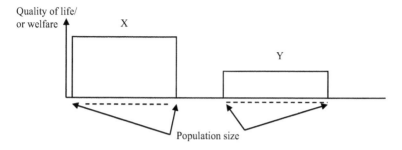

Figure 2.1

person in that population. The breadth of the rectangle illustrates the size of the population. So population X is the same size as population Y but members of population X have a higher quality of life than members of population Y. Strictly speaking, the lives that comprise these populations could have any spatial or temporal locations. For example, population X (or population Y, or both) could consist of many generations separated by many millions of miles. Basically though, it is easiest to assume that these populations consist of lives that comprise a single generation. This is easiest because any serious attempt to engage with the inevitable changes that occur in the context of welfare in populations that change across time adds a level of complexity that goes beyond our present remit.

By 'comparative' I mean *evaluative*: a comparison of which of some set of populations is *better* or *worse*. By *better* or *worse* here I mean better or worse in an 'all things considered' sense but I am only concerned with two ways in which populations can vary: the number of lives within them, and the welfare of those lives. This is important. There are many ways in which one population could be better or worse than another that I am factoring out. For example, one population may be *morally* superior to another if all those within it are engaged in some morally laudable task such as trying to fulfil their duty. Or one population may be aesthetically superior to another if the former realises some aesthetic end. This is not my concern when I discuss the comparison of populations. My concern is only with comparisons that concern population size and welfare distribution. Of course, facts about the distribution of welfare may be morally or aesthetically significant, but this, for present purposes, is not to the point.

This is relevant for thinking about the Repugnant Conclusion. Return to the summary given above by Parfit. It states that a population consisting of many billions lives all of which are barely worth living is better *all else equal* than a much smaller population consisting of much better lives.

The 'all else equal' clause is important. We could imagine that the enormous population of many billions are all engaged in a morally laudable endeavour or struggle, while those within the smaller population are not. Or we could imagine that the enormous population is *aesthetically* superior. Perhaps all of its members devote their lives to arranging themselves in a magnificent shape that can be seen from space, while the members of the smaller population mill around in an uninteresting fashion. If these were true, then perhaps the superiority of the much larger population would not be repugnant. Crucially though, all else would not be equal. Parfit's claim is the much more surprising one that that *all else being equal* the enormous population is superior.

So how, with our understandings of both 'population' and 'comparison' now in place, should we compare populations? We need to appeal to some kind of principle. Ideally, the principle would apply with perfect generality; it would allow us to compare *any* populations. Imagine all of the possible populations, where these can differ in terms of their size and the distribution of welfare amongst those in them. Ideally, a principle would allow us to rank all of these different populations in a list from best to worst, allowing that some may be equally good. We could call any such principle a *fully comprehensive* principle. Even more ideally than this, our principle would tell us *by how much* any population was better than any other; it would provide a cardinal, and not merely an ordinal, ranking of populations.[1]

Perhaps there is some such principle to be found, perhaps more likely not. We will return to this later. But let's simply begin optimistically by assuming that there is. What might it look like? There is an obvious candidate answer. Suppose that some lives are, or would be, good for those who live them. These are lives that 'have positive welfare' or 'have a positive quality of life', or as I shall sometimes simply say 'are good'. And suppose that some lives 'have negative welfare' or 'have a negative quality of life' or simply 'are bad'. An obvious candidate principle is that the goodness of the population is a sum of the positive welfare contained in all of the lives in it, minus the negative welfare. The more the resulting total, the better. That's how we do the comparison. How we work out what welfare itself is – that is, what properties lives have that make them good or bad, positive or negative – is another matter. Let's just set this to one side for now. We are, at present, really only interested in the form of the principle. And we now have a *very* simple candidate. I formulate it roughly below. In this formulation, I let 'α' and 'β' stand for populations. The specific populations that exemplify these in the various diagrams used above and below will be designated by ordinary capital letters (e.g. 'A', 'B', 'X', 'Y'). I shall refer to the principle as *Totalism*.

Totalism: For any populations, α and β, α is, all else equal, better than β if and only if the total sum of (positive and negative) welfare at α is greater than at β.

This principle is, of course, very crude: there are lots of contestable assumptions in play. I return to this below. But, in broad outline, it is also appealing. It is a simple, intuitive start-point. And importantly, for our purposes, it is all that we need to deduce the Repugnant Conclusion.[2] This is because a population of ten billion people, all of whom enjoy very high welfare, may yet contain *less* total welfare than a much larger population all of whom have lives of marginally positive level of welfare, provided that the second population is large enough. The following diagram illustrates the point (Figure 2.2).

At the left-hand side of the diagram, A represents a population that consists of ten billion lives of a very high level of welfare. Z represents a population in which each person enjoys only marginally positive welfare, but in which the population is sufficiently large (as indicated by the dotted line) that the total amount of welfare is greater than in A. We have arrived at the Repugnant Conclusion. The argument that we have used to get there is very simple. It can be represented as follows:

1. If Totalism is true, then the Repugnant Conclusion is true.
2. Totalism is true.
3. (1, 2) The Repugnant Conclusion is true.

This simple argument illustrates the simplest possible case for the Repugnant Conclusion. It requires modification (more on this below). It is a useful start-point nonetheless and even in this form it should make clear that at least one feature of Parfit's initial presentation of the Repugnant Conclusion – set out above – is inessential; his reference to *ten billion* people specifically. The point of the Repugnant Conclusion is a more general one. It is that for any perfectly equal population (that is, any population in

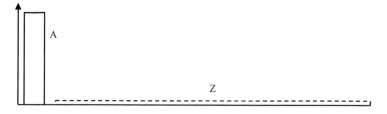

Figure 2.2

which all of those within it have the same quality of life or welfare as one another), where each life is of a very high level of welfare, there is a better – because much larger – population whose members all have lives that are only marginally positive. This alternative formulation appears in Parfit's more recent presentation:

> Compared with the existence of many people who would all have some very high quality of life, there is some much larger number of people whose existence would be better, even though these people would all have lives that are barely worth living.
>
> Parfit 2016: 110

This is the form of the Repugnant Conclusion that I shall work with in what follows.

The case for the Repugnant Conclusion does not rest solely on the argument given above. This will become clear later in this chapter when I provide some much stronger arguments for it. But the above argument is a good start-point nonetheless. It allows us to get a handle on the Repugnant Conclusion and bring out some of the assumptions that will be made in the rest of this book. Some require further justification than I can manage here. My aim is just to state them up-front.

Assumptions

Firstly, I am assuming that we can, in principle, make true evaluative judgments and that this isn't 'a mere matter of opinion'; I assume that they are the kinds of things that we can think and reason about, and about which some views might be – and are – wrong. This doesn't rule out many views: it is inconsistent only with the most extreme forms of moral relativism and error theory. As such this assumption may not sound terribly interesting. As we shall see in conclusion however, some of the arguments of this book may actually give us cause to revisit it.

Secondly, I shall assume that evaluative judgments are distinct from deontic judgments, and I shall focus on the former. Evaluative judgments are judgments about goodness or betterness. Deontic judgments are judgments about what people ought to do. In comparing different populations my concern is entirely evaluative. It concerns which population is better. It doesn't concern which population one ought to bring about (were one capable of doing so). This is a simplifying assumption. While some people – traditional consequentialists – think that the evaluative facts straightforwardly fix the deontic facts, many do not. Following most of the literature on comparing populations I shall limit my focus to evaluation.[3]

Thirdly, I shall largely ignore any questions about the identity of those who comprise the populations that I compare. I assume that we can compare populations *whoever* comprises them. In doing this, I am bypassing some contentious issues. One might suspect that for one population to be better than another, it must be better *for* someone. To think this would be to adhere to a (particular) version of what is often called a *person-affecting principle*. If it were true, it could seriously complicate the enterprise of comparing populations. Consider the following pair of populations, V and W (Figure 2.3).

In this diagram, one population, V, consists of a population in which each life has a high, positive welfare. The other population, W, is of the same size, though each life has a negative welfare ('zero' welfare is indicated by the horizontal line labelled 'the neutral level', more on which below). Clearly, V is better than W. But this is not obviously the case if the person-affecting principle is true. If the person-affecting principle were true, then, arguably, we could only conclude that V is better if at least one person exists in both V and W (as only then would V be better for someone). This should make clear how the truth of the person-affecting principle would complicate comparisons of populations: we could not compare unless we knew *who* lived in the comparator populations. The complications worsen if some variant on the person-affecting principle is true such that the welfare of those who exist in multiple populations receive extra *weighting*.[4] And they worsen further still depending on whether we are of the view that someone's existence can itself be better or worse for them than their non-existence.[5]

As it happens, I think that there are good reasons to reject the person-affecting principle. This allows us to avoid some of these complications.[6] But I shall simply ignore them in what follows. I shall assume that we can compare populations regardless of who comprises them. I shall follow the now-standard terminology in much of the contemporary literature by referring to the constituents of populations for the purposes of comparison as 'lives' rather 'people': what matters for comparative purposes is the lives

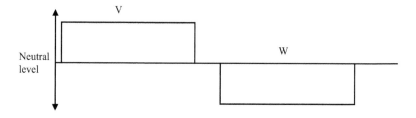

Figure 2.3

that comprise a population, not the identity of those who possess them ('the people'). So when, in subsequent sections, I refer to different populations that contain 'the same lives', I simply mean the same number, at the same welfare-level, which does not entail the very same individuals.

I should acknowledge from the start that my decision to set aside 'person affecting' considerations will cause some readers get off the boat early on. There is a – quite understandable – tradition of scepticism about non-person-affecting approaches to the comparison of populations (and morality more generally). Complementing this, there are person-affecting frameworks for the comparison of populations: frameworks designed to be sensitive to the kinds of worries for simple person-affecting views as sketched above.[7] I regret that I can't engage in detail with these here.

Fourthly, I shall assume that some lives are better or worse than others. By 'good', 'bad' and 'neutral' here I don't mean *morally* good, bad or neutral. I mean good, bad or neutral in terms of what we might call prudential value, or welfare. So I am assuming that some lives are better or worse than others in terms of their welfare. The diagrams – and interpretations of them – presented above clearly rely on this assumption. For example, members of V have a better quality of life than members of W. This is a contestable assumption. There is a tradition of *rejecting* so-called *inter-personal comparisons of welfare*.[8] Those who deny that there can be inter-personal comparisons of welfare deny that we can truly say of two lives that one is better than another (the basic rationale is that there is no common metric that we could use to make such a comparison). If the comparisons of populations that are the subject-matter of this book are to make sense, this must be false: it must be possible to make inter-personal welfare comparisons. I shall simply assume that we can do this.

Fifthly, I shall assume that lives can be good or bad *in an absolute sense*: some people enjoy a level of welfare such that their lives are good, whereas others have lives that are bad. This assumption is perhaps clearest in the example involving V and W above. This is an example in which some lives are good and some are bad. There is a level – *the neutral level* – between these at which lives would be neither good nor bad. Lives just above this have *marginally positive welfare* or are *marginally good*. Lives just below it have *marginally negative welfare* or are *marginally bad*. This assumption is at work in the Repugnant Conclusion itself. The Repugnant Conclusion compares a population of high-quality lives with a population of lives that are 'barely worth living'. These are lives that have marginally positive welfare. The reason for making this assumption (about the existence of absolute quality of life) is that we need it to deal with specific cases. Suppose that you knew that, if you brought someone into existence they would be tortured terribly for a short period of time and then die. Their life would be entirely characterised by the most terrible pain. It would be devoid of happiness or meaning. Should you – if you are thinking only about the welfare of that person – bring them into existence? Clearly, the answer is 'no'. The answer is 'no' because of the quality of life that this person would have; it would be bad. Unless we can make claims about the absolute welfare, then we could not say this.

Sixthly, and relatedly, I am – for now – assuming that we can aggregate the total amount of welfare across different lives allowing us to say that one population contains more, less, or the same amount of total welfare as another. This is a highly contestable assumption given issues with inter-personal welfare comparison as noted above. I shall assume for the present that we can do this, but in fact this assumption will be shown to be somewhat dispensable in later sections of this chapter. In a closely related assumption about the structure of welfare, I am also assuming that welfare levels are ordered in such a way that one welfare level can be *only marginally* better or worse than another. This is somewhat controversial and has been a subject of recent interest.[9]

Seventhly, I am largely assuming that many of the issues that are particularly troubling in the context of real-world population growth can be set to one side. I am assuming, for example, that it is possible for there to be an enormous population of lives that are barely worth living of the kind described in the Repugnant Conclusion. In the real world, this may not be the case. Perhaps, for example, sufficiently large real-world populations would be simply unsustainable: resource limitations may be insufficient to support them. I will largely set these kinds of concerns to one side. My concern is with the highly abstract question of how to compare populations on the assumption that there are, as economists say, no 'externalities': no limitations to resource, no inevitable conflict as a result of over-population and so on. Relatedly, as mentioned above, I will generally also assume for most of what follows that a population is simply a single generation: that all of those who live in it live at the same time and die at the time and that the future is not a concern. This is another simplifying idealisation that will make my task easier. Many readers will find this frustrating. They will want to think about 'real world' issues rather than the abstractions that are the subject of this book. In part, my response to these readers is simply that my concern differs from theirs. I am interested in the nature of the good. That just is an abstract philosophical question, and it is a question of significant interest in its own right. There is, however, a practical response (to those who are so inclined). If we cannot answer the highly simplified questions about the relative goodness of populations that we are considering here – and I shall show that arguably we cannot – then what chance have we of tackling the extremely messy version of them that we find around us in the real world? Very little.

There is much more that could be said about the assumptions that I am making, and there are many more assumptions being made. I shall return to some of them in due course.

2.2 Alternatives to Totalism

In the previous section, I presented a basic argument for the Repugnant Conclusion. It was based on a very general principle for comparing populations. According to that principle:

> *Totalism*: For any populations, α and β, α is, all else equal, better than β if and only if the total sum of (positive and negative) welfare at α is greater than at β.[10]

One might reasonably doubt whether this should make us accept the Repugnant Conclusion. After all, Totalism is, quite independently, far from uncontroversial. Indeed, it is arguably less secure than the falsity of the conclusion (the Repugnant Conclusion) that it entails. As I mentioned above, I don't think that Totalism *is* the strongest base for the Repugnant Conclusion. I present much stronger arguments later in this chapter. It is these that I will be reliant on, not the argument from Totalism. I do think, however, that the Totalist argument for the Repugnant Conclusion should not be dismissed too lightly, not least because some of those who have accepted or been troubled by the Repugnant Conclusion – including some who we examine at greater length in later chapters – have taken this kind of argument seriously. It is worth saying something more about why. That is the aim of this sub-section.

One of the key reasons – arguably the key reason – for taking Totalism seriously is that despite its weaknesses, none of the obvious alternatives fare any better. Compared to the obvious alternative candidate fully comprehensive principles, Totalism actually looks quite good. This doesn't show that it is true. There may be no fully comprehensive principle. Or perhaps any such principle is fabulously complex. But let's again be optimistic and work with the assumption that there is a principle to be found here, and that it displays the kind of level of simplicity that is characteristic of powerful general laws. What, if we do this, are the alternatives to Totalism? I very briefly outline the problems with four of the major contenders. Experienced readers familiar with these views and the objections to them may skip ahead.[11]

Averagism

One obvious alternative is to rank populations on the basis of average welfare. According to this principle:

> *Averagism*: For any populations, α and β, α is, all else equal, better than β if and only if average welfare at α is greater than at β.

This is an obvious alternative because it avoids the Repugnant Conclusion. Consider once again the diagram used to illustrate the Repugnant Conclusion (below). The average quality of life is higher at A than at Z (Figure 2.4):

One might think that this makes Averagism a better candidate principle than Totalism, but this is questionable. Averagism faces serious problems of its own. It entails that, in some cases, it would be better to add any number of people whose lives are *bad* than to add some number of people whose lives are good.[12] This is typically referred to as *The Sadistic Conclusion* and is fairly unquestionably incorrect. To see how Averagism entails the Sadistic Conclusion consider the following diagram, consisting of populations T and U (Figure 2.5):

T is a population comprised of two sub-populations (as indicated by the arrows) in which a large population of happy people is supplemented by the

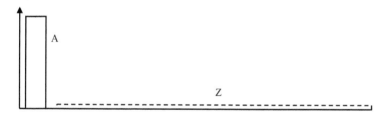

Figure 2.4

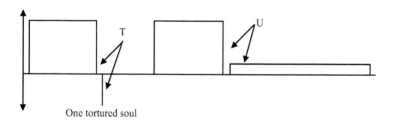

One tortured soul

Figure 2.5

addition of one very bad life. In U, the same population of happy people is supplemented by the addition of a very large number of people who lead good lives. Which is better T or U? Clearly, U is better. But if Averagism is true, then – provided the example is set-up in the right way – T is better. This is because, if the supplementary population is large enough at U, the average welfare will be lowered more than it would be by the addition of one tortured soul at T. One useful way to see this is by assigning numbers to populations and levels of welfare.[13] Suppose that the basic population held in common between T and U consists of 10 lives each with welfare-level of 10. Average welfare is 10. Suppose that the one supplementary life at T has welfare-level –1. Average welfare is now just under 10. Suppose that the supplementary sub-population at U consists of 100 lives, each with welfare-level 8. Average welfare is now a shade over 8. So average welfare is higher at T. So Averagism licenses the Sadistic Conclusion. We can represent the argument as follows:

1. If Averagism is true, then the Sadistic Conclusion is true.
2. The Sadistic Conclusion isn't true.
3. (1, 2) Averagism isn't true.

Diminishing-Value View

Consider another alternative fully comprehensive principle: the *Diminishing-Value View*. This is a modification of Totalism designed to avoid the Repugnant Conclusion.[14] Totalism, recall, makes the goodness of a population a simple sum of the welfare of all its lives. This is its simplicity and its strength, but it is also the feature of it that yields the Repugnant Conclusion: it is because of this that the more people there are, provided that their lives are worth living, the better the population will be; potentially without limit. The Diminishing-Value View effectively imposes a limit to prevent this potentially infinite accumulation of goodness, thereby avoiding the Repugnant Conclusion. On the Diminishing-Value View, the goodness of the population is a *decreasing function* of the welfares of all its lives. This means that as the size of the population increases, the contribution that each life's welfare makes to the total goodness of the population decreases. It is a consequence of this that the total goodness of a popualtion tends towards a limit in the way that, for example, the function represented by $1+1/2 + 1/4 + 1/8 \ldots$ tends towards 2. According to this view as I shall understand it:

> *Diminishing-Value View*: For any populations, α and β, α is, all else equal, better than β if and only if the sum of an appropriate function of

welfares of lives at α is greater than the sum of the same function of the welfares of the lives at β.

There are various ways of describing the 'appropriate' function. We will want to do so in such a way that we can avoid the Repugnant Conclusion. Perhaps the most obvious – but not the only – way to do this is to allow the limit to which the goodness of a population tends to be determined by the *average* welfare of the population.[15] This allows us to avoid the Repugnant Conclusion because the limit to which the goodness of a population will tend is 'capped' by its average welfare. The result is that there is a limit to how good a population can be, no matter how many lives it contains. That limit is low for populations comprised of only marginally positive lives, such as those lives 'at Z' in the Repugnant Conclusion. It is higher for populations comprised of much better lives, such as those lives 'at A' in the Repugnant Conclusion. We can represent this in the following diagram (Figure 2.6):

So the Diminishing-Value View looks appealing. But it too faces serious problems: problems that should make us question whether it is any better than Totalism. One problem is that it entails that the *badness* of a population tend towards a limit too. Consider a population that consists of a large number of lives that are very bad or not worth living. If the Diminishing-Value View is correct, then as we add more of these lives to the population, the badness of the population tends towards a limit; that given by their average badness. This is illustrated in the following diagram (Figure 2.7):

This consequence of the Diminishing-Value View seems wrong. A world gets worse and worse as the number of bad lives at it increases. It does not tend to a limit in this way. So the following simple argument is sound.

1. If the Diminishing-Value View is true, then a population's badness tends to a limit as the number of bad lives increases.
2. A population's badness does not tend to a limit as the number of bad lives increases.
3. (1, 2) The Diminishing-Value View isn't true.

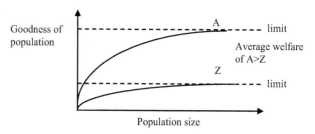

Figure 2.6

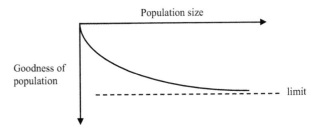

Figure 2.7

A defender of the Diminishing-Value View could respond by introducing an asymmetry between the evaluation of populations of *good* lives and *bad* lives: only the former tend towards a limit. This would allow for rejection of the first premise. Clearly though, this is a theoretically unsatisfying ad hoc modification.

There is a second important argument against the Diminishing-Value View: it lacks adequate philosophical foundation. Why would the number of people already alive matter for the amount of goodness that any given person's welfare would contribute to the population? Surely the amount of goodness that any given person's welfare would add to the population is determined entirely by how much welfare that life contains; by the quality of that person's life. And surely someone's quality of life is not intrinsically dependent on the size of the population (though of course it may be contingently dependent given the fact that resources may be limited). So surely the contribution that any given person's welfare would make to the goodness of a population is not (intrinsically) dependent on the size of the population. This is of course consistent with population size having an effect on quality of life in virtue so-called 'externalities'; limited resources and the like.

Critical Level/Band View

A third alternative to Totalism is from *Critical-Level* or *Critical-Band* views. *Critical-Level* is simpler.[16] According to *Critical-Level Views*, there is a threshold or cut-off level of welfare such that only those lives that reach that threshold make a positive contribution to the goodness of the population. This allows us to avoid the Repugnant Conclusion. Consider the diagram below. In this diagram, only those lives that have a level of welfare above the threshold make a positive contribution to the goodness of the world. Those below do not. So the lives at Z do not. So Z does not have a higher total goodness than A. So the Repugnant Conclusion is avoided. We can represent this as follows (Figure 2.8):

Here, the total welfare at A above the threshold is higher than the total welfare at Z above the threshold. So A is better. So the Repugnant Conclusion is avoided. The principle being used can be represented as follows:

> *Underspecified Critical-Level View*: For any populations, α and β, and some positive threshold welfare level, α is, all else equal, better than β if the sum of the welfare of those at α above the threshold level is greater than that of the sum of the welfare of those at β above the threshold level.

As roughly presented above, the Critical-Level View is underspecified. It is underspecified because are not told how to value lives below the threshold level; it does not tell us how to factor these lives into a comparison. There are several options. One option is that all lives below the threshold make *zero* contribution to the goodness of the population; they make it neither worse nor better. A second option is that all lives below the threshold make *negative* contributions to the goodness of the population; they make it worse. A third option is that lives that fall between the neutral level and the threshold make zero contribution to the goodness of the population, and lives that fall below the neutral level make a negative contribution. None of these are good options. Begin by thinking about the first option. This is obviously implausible. It entails that adding lives of negative welfare would not make the population worse. This is clearly false. Just to be clear, the argument is:

1. If the Critical-Level (first interpretation) View is true, then adding terrible lives doesn't make the population worse in any way.
2. Adding terrible lives does make the population worse in some way.
3. (1, 2) The Critical-Level (first interpretation) View is false.

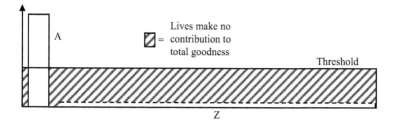

Figure 2.8

The second option is also pretty obviously false. It is implausible because – much as we saw with Averagism – it entails *The Sadistic Conclusion*. The diagram below illustrates (Figure 2.9).

The interpretation of the critical level view that we are considering entails that R could be worse than S. This will be the case if the total amount of welfare in R is large enough, given that all of this welfare will make a negative contribution to the goodness of the population. This is highly counter-intuitive: R contains only good lives whereas S contains only bad lives. The interpretation of the Critical-Level View that we are considering must be false. The argument is as follows:

1. If the Critical-Level (second interpretation) View is true, then the Sadistic Conclusion is true.
2. The Sadistic Conclusion is not true.
3. (1, 2) The Critical-Level (second interpretation) View is false.

According to the third option, there is a 'band' of welfare between the threshold and the neutral level such that lives that fall in this band make no contribution to the value of the world, but below which they make a negative contribution. This is really a specific instance of a more general view, the *Critical-Band View*. The lower limit of the band could be set at the neutral level (as I have assumed here), or it could be set at some alternative below the neutral level as the diagram below represents (Figure 2.10).

This diagram illustrates how the Critical-Band View allows us to avoid the Repugnant Conclusion. We can represent the principle that is being used roughly as follows:

> *Critical-Band View*: For any populations, α and β, and some threshold welfare levels, one positive, one negative, α is, all else equal, better than β if the sum of the welfare of those at α above the positive threshold, minus the sum of the negative welfare of the members of α below

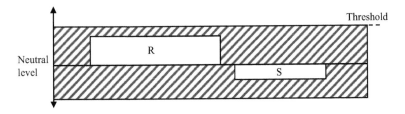

Figure 2.9

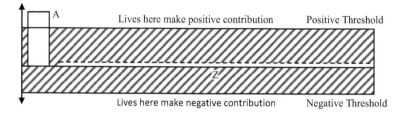

Figure 2.10

the negative threshold, is greater than the same sum of the (positive and negative welfares above and below the two thresholds) of those at β.

Although promising, this view is problematic in virtue of both its counter-intuitive consequences and its lack of philosophical rationale. The obvious counter-intuitive consequence is that two lives that differ in their levels of welfare can nonetheless make the very same contribution to the goodness of the population. This seems clearly false. Consider the following diagram comparing populations P and Q (Figure 2.11).

In this diagram, those at P have good lives, just below the positive threshold whereas those at Q have lives just above the negative threshold. Which is a better population? If the Critical-Band View is correct, we should be indifferent between them. But clearly, we shouldn't: P is better. So the Critical-Band View is false. The argument is as follows:

1. If the Critical-Band View is true, then populations with welfare levels just below the positive threshold and those with welfare levels just above the negative threshold are equally good.
2. They aren't.
3. (1, 2) The Critical-Band view is false.

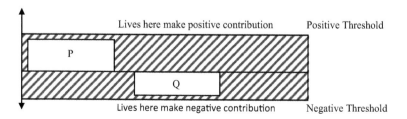

Figure 2.11

The philosophical problem is that it is unclear that there is a good rationale for setting thresholds at non-zero levels. The overwhelmingly obvious rationale for drawing a threshold somewhere is that that lives above that threshold are good. This mandates drawing a threshold at the neutral level: lives above it make positive contribution, lives below it make a negative contribution. This is just Totalism, not a Critical-Band (or level) View. Setting a threshold *elsewhere* – as defenders of the Critical-Band (or Critical-Level) View do – would be peculiar. Suppose, to illustrate, that we are interested in how wealthy a nation is. We find that the combined wealth held by all members of that nation sums to $1 trillion. Now suppose that, altering nothing else, we add an extra person to the nation and that this person has total wealth of $100. Should we conclude that that the total wealth of the nation has increased, or that it remains exactly the same? Clearly, it has increased. It has increased by $100. Now suppose that someone were to object. Suppose that they were to say: Only additions of amounts of money greater than $200 contribute positively to a nation's total wealth. This would be a bizarre thing to say. Although crude in some respects, at the level of underlying philosophical rationale, the Critical-Band (or Critical-Level) Views seem troublingly analogous.

Lexical-Priority View

Despite the fact that drinking a cup of tea always contributes something to one's welfare, no number of cups of tea can contribute more to one's welfare than winning an Olympic gold medal. There is a difference in kind between the value of drinking a cup of tea and winning Olympic gold. The latter has lexical priority over the former. We can apply this plausible thought to the comparison of populations. According to the resulting view, all lives with positive welfare make a positive contribution to the goodness of the world, and all lives with negative welfare make a negative contribution, but there is nevertheless some cut-off or threshold welfare-level such that no increase in the total amount of welfare below this threshold can compensate for the higher quality above it.[17] Welfare above the threshold is of the superior kind. The following diagram very simply illustrates how this approach can allow us to avoid the Repugnant Conclusion (Figure 2.12):[18]

Here, the threshold falls between the welfare levels of those at A and at Z. This prevents the Repugnant Conclusion. It does so because no number of lives that fall below the threshold – including lives at Z – can compensate for the superior quality of life above that threshold (at A). We can understand this view very roughly as follows:

> *Underspecified Lexical-Priority View*: For any populations, α and β, and some threshold welfare level, α is, all else equal, better than β if α

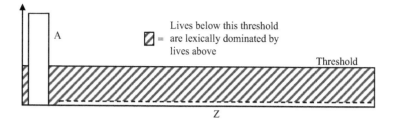

Figure 2.12

contains some lives at or above that threshold level but β contains no lives at or above it.

This is under-specified in a number of respects; most obviously that it doesn't tell us how to compare populations in which no lives are above the lexical threshold, nor does it tell us how to compare populations that combine lives above and below the lexical threshold. There are lots of different ways of filling this detail in. But however we do it, there are counter-intuitive consequences for a Lexical-Priority View. Consider the following two diagrams:

The diagram represents two populations. The first, M, consists of one life at the lexical threshold and a great many very miserable lives. The second, N, consists of many lives just below the lexical threshold. The Lexical-Priority View entails, counter-intuitively, that M is better than N. The argument is (Figure 2.13):

1. If the Lexical-Priority View is true, then any population with one life at the lexical threshold is better than any population with no lives at it.

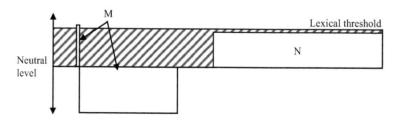

Figure 2.13

2. A population with one life at the lexical threshold and many lives of misery is worse than a population with no lives at the lexical threshold.
3. (1, 2) The Lexical-Priority View is false.

It is possible to modify the Lexical-Priority View to avoid this result by adding a *second* lexical threshold. This threshold is set at the neutral level so that no amount of welfare above it can compensate for any amount below: avoiding negative welfare takes lexical priority over all other alternatives.

This view avoids the problem sketched above but it is highly dubious. Firstly, it entails that a population that consists of one life just below the negative threshold and a great many lives far above the positive threshold is worse than a population consisting of an enormous number of positive lives just below the positive threshold. This seems clearly wrong. One could attempt to add more lexical thresholds to remedy this. But rather than resolving the problem by adding more lexical thresholds, we simply increase the ease with which we can generate counter-intuitive conclusions. There is a second more fundamental problem facing Lexical-Priority Views. It concerns the use of a threshold. Imagine some life exactly at the positive threshold. Any lessening in the quality of life would take them below the threshold. Suppose this is a consequence of their life containing some good, such as – to take a plausible candidate – a sufficiently high degree of meaning in life. Now imagine a second individual. This individual has a life that is otherwise indistinguishable from that of the first individual, but that is less meaningful to the smallest possible degree.[19] This second individual's life falls below the threshold. So no number of lives that are exactly as good as that of the second individual can be as good as that of the first. Although not impossible, this is an extremely puzzling result: its philosophical rationale is hard to find.[20]

Conclusion

Totalism entails the Repugnant Conclusion. Totalism may not seem like an attractive view at first. However, when compared with other candidate comprehensive principles it looks rather better. It is philosophically well-motivated: the claim that the more there is of what's good and the less of what's bad, the better, is easy to motivate and hard to deny. And although it is vulnerable to counter-intuitive consequences, so are the competitors.

Despite this, I don't think that Totalism is the best motivation for the Repugnant Conclusion. There are well-known better motivations that come from non-comprehensive principles that are much harder to reject. I present two of these motivations below. My aim is to present the arguments in a readable and intuitive fashion that allows us to properly engage with a specific response – the *Quality of Life Strategy* – in the next section.

2.3 Continuum Reasoning

One way of reaching the Repugnant Conclusion is via what I shall refer to as *Continuum Reasoning*.[21] We can represent it in the following diagram (Figure 2.14):

In this diagram, we begin with a population, A, consisting of a small number of very high-quality lives. There is a better population with a marginally lower quality of life, provided that the number enjoying that life is sufficiently large. This is population B. Similarly, there is a better population than B in which a marginally lower quality of life is compensated for by a sufficiently large increase in the number enjoying that life. Call that population C. We can continue this until we reach Z. The result – assuming transitivity of betterness (more on which below) is that Z is better than A. This is *The Repugnant Conclusion*. We have arrived at it via a version of a principle that is now commonly referred to as 'Quantity'.[22]

> *Quantity*: For any populations, α and β, both of which consist of lives at positive, perfectly equal welfare-levels, if the welfare-level at β is only marginally lower than at α, then, if β has a sufficiently greater population than α, then, all else equal, β is better.

The argument we are using is as follows:

1. If Quantity is true, then the Repugnant Conclusion is true.
2. Quantity is true
3. (1, 2) The Repugnant Conclusion is true.

On a first pass, Quantity may appear to be simply a variant on Totalism. But it is much weaker and so is not vulnerable to many of the criticisms of

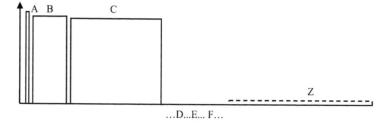

...D...E... F...

Figure 2.14

Totalism. I illustrate three. Firstly, Totalism entails that a lowering of the average quality of life in a population will always be compensated by an increase in the population size, provided that this 'trade-off' increases total welfare. This is a strong assumption. It entails that there is no limit to the loss in quality of life that cannot be compensated for, provided enough lives are added. One might reasonably be sceptical of this kind of 'easy' compensation. Quantity does not rely on this. Quantity relies on the much weaker assumption that losses in quality of life *can* be compensated by gains in quantity, provided that the losses in quality are *marginal*, and the gains in quantity are *sufficiently large*. This is much weaker than Totalism, and so much less objectionable.

Secondly, Totalism has some unsavoury consequences with respect to populations that contain lives of negative welfare. Quantity avoids these consequences. If Totalism is true, then the goodness of a population is determined by the sum of positive and negative welfares. This entails what is sometimes called *The Very Repugnant Conclusion*.[23] The Very Repugnant Conclusion is the view that populations comprised of many bad lives can be better than populations comprised of a lot of great lives, provided that alongside the bad lives there is a sufficiently large number of lives barely worth living. This is illustrated in the diagram below (Figure 2.15).

In this diagram, A represents a population comprised only of great lives whereas Z* represents a population comprised of a large number of very bad lives and an enormous number of lives of marginally positive welfare. If Totalism is true then, provided the number of marginally good lives is enormous enough Z* is better. This illustrates the Very Repugnant Conclusion. It is hard to swallow. Totalism entails it but Quantity does not. There are several reasons for this. One is that Quantity makes no claims about populations containing *negative* welfare lives. Another is that Quantity only makes claims about how to compare *perfectly equal* populations (of which the second diagram is not an example). There are some interesting issues as regards whether the underlying rationale for Quantity – whatever it may be – can avoid these commitments. I believe it can. I return to this in Chapter 4.

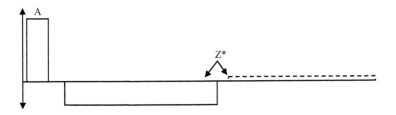

Figure 2.15

Thirdly, it is worth noting that Quantity can be – and as I have presented it *is* – formulated so as to avoid the commitment that Totalism makes to the existence of facts about the *total welfare* of a population. According to Totalism, the goodness of a population is determined by the total welfare of that population. This implies that there is such a thing; that it is possible to sum the welfares of different lives within a population to a total welfare. As I mentioned in 2.1, one might reasonably be sceptical of this. If so, one will be sceptical of Totalism. As I have formulated it though, Quantity contains no such reference. It merely refers to populations of differing numbers of lives, each of which is (internally) perfectly equal, though both of which have marginally different welfare levels from each other. Of course, if one wanted to, one could add in a reference to total welfare. In some older formulations, this is included. But it is not included in now-standard formulations, especially those due to Arrhenius. I have followed this.[24]

Quantity is much harder to deny than Totalism. However, unlike Totalism, it isn't a candidate for being a fully comprehensive principle. It doesn't tell us how to rank all populations. It only tells us how to rank that subset of populations that contain only positive welfare lives at perfectly equal levels, separated from one another by a marginal amount. This makes Quantity less powerful than Totalism. But it doesn't thereby make it less likely to be true.

Transitivity

As I have presented it above, the Continuum Argument for the Repugnant Conclusion proceeds via the application of Quantity. More precisely though, an additional principle is also required: the transitivity of betterness. According to a simple version of this principle applied specifically to populations:

> *Transitivity*: For any populations α, β, χ, if α is better than β and β is better than χ, then α is better than χ.

Without this, the Continuum Argument would not go through. This is because without it the fact that – in the Continuum Argument – B is better than A and C is better than B would not entail that C (and so D, E, F and ultimately Z) is better than A. So, really, the Continuum Argument is as follows:

1. If Quantity and Transitivity are true, then the Repugnant Conclusion is true.
2. Quantity and Transitivity are true
3. (1, 2) The Repugnant Conclusion is true.

In fact, it is possible to make use of variants on Transitivity in the context of the argument for the Repugnant Conclusion. I shall briefly summarise two here. Both are summarised because they represent ways in which the case for the Repugnant Conclusion can be made more compelling. The first variant concerns the transitivity of a weaker property than betterness: namely, at-least-as-good-as-ness. According to this principle:

Transitivity (at least as good as): For any populations α, β, χ, if α is at least as good as β and β is at least as good as χ, then α is at least as good as χ.

This is no less compelling than the simple version of Transitivity. But it is relevant because if we work with it we can weaken – and so make more compelling – Quantity. Specifically, we can work with a version of Quantity according to which β is *not worse than* α. According to this version of Quantity:

Quantity (Not worse): For any populations, α and β, both of which consist of lives at positive, perfectly equal welfare-levels, if the welfare-level at β is only marginally lower than at α, then, if β has a sufficiently greater population than α, then, all else equal, β is *not worse*.

This is even harder to deny than Quantity. The second variant on Transitivity that we could use weakens *it* (rather than allowing us to weaken Quantity). It states that if one population is better than another and a third is better still, then the third is *not worse* than the first.

Transitivity (Weakened): For any populations α, β, χ, if α is better than β and β is better than χ, then α is not worse than χ.

This is an extremely weak principle – significantly weaker than the original version of Transitivity presented above. This is important because it can go some way towards assuaging existing worries about the status of Transitivity within the axiological literature: worries that exist given the existence of some counter-examples to an unrestricted version of strong forms of Transitivity.[25] This comes with two caveats. Firstly, and most importantly, I should grant that it will probably not go far enough. Worries with the transitivity of betterness (and related properties) runs deep. A full engagement with these arguments is beyond the scope of this short monograph, and could present a radically different response to the puzzles of population and much else besides, potentially rendering the Quality of

Life Strategy redundant. Secondly, if we *do* accept this weakened version of Transitivity, then we will have to make a minor modification to the Repugnant Conclusion itself (if it is to be derivable via a Continuum Argument). The weakened version of Transitivity would only allow us to conclude that, in the Continuum Argument, Z is *not worse than* A. This isn't *quite* the Repugnant Conclusion. According to the Repugnant Conclusion, Z is *better than* A. It is a weakened version that we can refer to as the *Weakened Repugnant Conclusion*. Surely though, this weakened conclusion is sufficiently similar to the Repugnant Conclusion for our purposes: anyone who is troubled by the Repugnant Conclusion would surely be (almost) equally perturbed by the Weakened Repugnant Conclusion. Consider a small population of the very best lives. Now consider an enormous population of lives that are only marginally good. Anyone who is uncomfortable with admitting the superiority of the latter population would surely also be uncomfortable to admit to indifference between the two.

Having presented these two variants on Transitivity, I shall – for ease of presentation – largely ignore them in what follows. My subsequent presentations will simply work with Quantity, Transitivity and the Repugnant Conclusion in their basic forms.

2.4 Dominance-Addition Reasoning

To this point, I have presented two ways of reasoning to the Repugnant Conclusion: via Totalism and via the Continuum Argument. In this section, I introduce a third type of argument: the *Dominance-Addition Argument*. I begin with an initial version – the *Mere-Addition Argument* – before showing that we can strengthen its appeal by weakening the assumptions on which it is based, thereby generating the Dominance-Addition Argument. Arguments of this form were first presented by Parfit in *Reasons and Persons* but there have been many variants since. I should acknowledge that my formulations do not precisely follow any of these presentations, but take elements from many of them, with intuitive appeal and readability in mind.[26] I should also acknowledge that there is now a significant literature concerning various ways in which the principles used in these formulations can be weakened in order to make them harder to refute. Much of this owes to Gustaf Arrhenius. Arrhenius has developed weakened versions of the principles presented below that dispense with many of the more contestable assumptions that I shall be making. In this chapter, I do not present Arrhenius's somewhat more technical – though undoubtedly more effective – up-dating of the basic argument, though I do return to it in Chapter 4 when we go into the details in a bit more depth.

Preliminary version: Simple Mere-Addition Reasoning

Consider the following diagram, which represents the three stages of the Mere-Addition Argument for the Repugnant Conclusion (Figure 2.16).[27]

In this diagram, we begin with a population, A. At the first stage, we improve A by moving to B. B is a population in which the A-lives are supplemented by some additional lives, all of which enjoy positive welfare. B is better than, or at least not worse than A, via the following principle:

> *Mere-Addition Principle*: For any populations, α and β, if α consists of lives at a positive, equal welfare-level, and β consists of the same lives, plus any number of additional lives at a marginally positive welfare-level, then, all else equal, β is better.

In the second stage, we move from B to Z. Z is a very large population in which each life is only marginally better than the less well-off lives at B. But, given the large population at Z, its total welfare is much higher than B's. Z is also, clearly, a much more equal population than B. So Z is better than Z based on the following principle:

> *Non-Anti-Egalitarianism (Preliminary)*: For any populations, α and β, if β is more equal than α and contains more total welfare than α, then β is, all else equal, better.

These principles are somewhat compelling: more so than Totalism. Nevertheless, I label the second of these principles 'preliminary' as it will be shown below that it can be made significantly weaker and hence significantly more compelling.

In the third stage, we add transitivity (I won't repeat the discussion of this principle from the previous section, but similar remarks apply). The result is

Figure 2.16

that Z is better than A. This is the Repugnant Conclusion. The argument that we have used to get there is as follows:

1. If the Mere-Addition Principle, Non-Anti-Egalitarianism (Preliminary) and Transitivity are true, then the Repugnant Conclusion is true.
2. The Mere Addition Principle, Non-Anti-Egalitarianism (Preliminary) and Transitivity are true.
3. (1, 2) The Repugnant Conclusion is true.

This is very different from both the Totalism and Continuum-Reasoning-based approaches. In what follows, I attempt to make it *much more* compelling by weakening the assumptions on which it is based.

Better version: Dominance-Addition Reasoning

There is a better version of this argument. I shall refer to it as the Dominance-Addition Argument.[28] It is something of a hybrid between the Mere-Addition Reasoning outlined above and the Continuum Reasoning used in 2.3 above. It allows us to deduce the Repugnant Conclusion via a multi-step argument that works by repeated use of much weaker versions of both the Mere-Addition Principle and Non-Anti-Egalitarianism, as well as Transitivity. It can be represented diagrammatically as follows (Figure 2.17):

We begin by moving from A to A$^+$. We do so by improving the welfare of those at A, and adding some new lives with welfare-level just below the welfare level of those at A. This improves the population via a modified version of the Mere-Addition Principle: the Dominance-Addition Principle. According to this principle:

> *Dominance-Addition Principle*: For any populations, α and β, if α consists of lives at a positive, equal welfare-level, and β consists of the same number of lives, but at a higher welfare-level, plus some other lives at any positive welfare-level, then β is, all else equal, better.

The Dominance-Addition Principle is weaker – and hence more compelling - than the Mere-Addition Principle in two ways. Yet (as we shall see) the Repugnant Conclusion is still derivable using it. The first respect in which the Dominance-Addition Principle is weaker is that the A-lives are actually *improved* on moving from A to A$^+$ (rather than remaining of the same quality, as in the Mere-Addition Principle). This modification will make the resulting principle much more compelling. How could improving some lives and worsening none not, all else equal, improve the population?

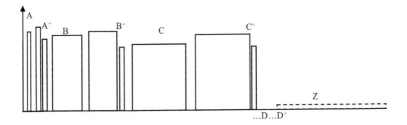

Figure 2.17

The second respect in which the Dominance-Addition Principle is weaker is that it allows that the new lives that we add in moving from A to A⁺ need not be at a marginally positive welfare level. They could be much better than this (as they are in diagram above). This is much weaker than the Mere-Addition Principle in which the lives that we add on moving from A to A⁺ are lives of marginally positive welfare. So the Dominance-Addition Principle is weaker than the Mere-Addition Principle in two ways and hence more compelling.

The Dominance-Addition Principle states that the population improves on moving from A to A⁺. We now apply a version of Non-Anti-Egalitarianism to show that the population improves in moving from A⁺ to B. There are lots of modifications that we could use to this end. The aim is to use the weakest and so most compelling that allows us to derive the Repugnant Conclusion. According to one version owing to Huemer, we can modify it so as to include a claim about improvement of *average* welfare, which weakens the principle and so renders it more compelling: surely one population is better than another, all else equal, if it has a higher total welfare, average welfare, and is more equal. The principle states:

> *Non-Anti-Egalitarianism*: For any populations, α and β, both of which consist of positive-welfare lives, if β is more equal than α and contains both more total welfare *and has a higher average welfare*, then β is, all else equal, better.[29]

This can be used to derive the Repugnant Conclusion: the level of B can be set so that it has a higher total welfare *and* average welfare than that of A+. This will be the case provided that the welfare-level at B is sufficiently higher than the welfare-level of the least well-off group at A⁺. Consider a very simple example by way of illustration. Suppose that A is a population consisting of one person with a welfare-level of 100. Now suppose that A^+ is a population of two lives, one with welfare-level 101 and one with welfare-level 95. By Dominance-Addition, A^+ is better than A. Now suppose that B is a population of two in which each life has welfare-level 99. By Non-Anti-Egalitarianism, B is better than A^+: B has a higher total welfare (198 to 196), a higher average welfare (99 to 98) and is more equal.

For present purposes, I think this is probably the most useful presentation of Non-Anti-Egalitarianism. I shall largely work with it in what follows. As I noted above, however, there are significantly weaker versions of recognisably similar principles that can nevertheless be used to derive the Repugnant Conclusion, owing primarily to Gustaf Arrhenius.[30] Arrhenius provides versions that he refers to as the *Inequality Aversion Condition* and *Non-Elitism* respectively (the latter being weaker than the former). These allow us to, amongst other things, avoid commitment to the summation of individual welfares ('total welfare') in the formulation of the principle. I will return to this in more detail in Chapter 4. But in order to get the view 'on the table' and for the purposes of presentation of the Quality of Life Strategy (the primary aim of the next chapter), we do not need to engage with these issues here. The simple presentation above is a clear and easily motivated start-point.

In addition to these two principles, we must also use a transitivity principle. This is necessary in order to allow us to infer from the superiority of B over A^+ and of A^+ over A to the superiority of B over A. Similar remarks apply to this principle as were made in discussion of the Continuum Argument earlier in this chapter.

This is perhaps the most compelling form of argument for the Repugnant Conclusion (although as we shall see in Chapter 4, even weaker and more compelling renderings of its principles can be provided). The Dominance-Addition Principle effectively claims that improving everyone's lot and adding some more people who are happy – and not much less happy than the others – doesn't necessarily make things worse, all else being equal. Non-Anti-Egalitarianism claims that simultaneously improving equality and increasing both the total and the average welfare improves the population. These are very compelling. And yet together they entail the Repugnant Conclusion.

2.5 Conclusion

Three different arguments for the Repugnant Conclusion have been presented. They have been presented in order of increasing plausibility. The first is based on a simple comprehensive principle that, although problematic in some respects, arguably fares as well as alternative candidate comprehensive principles. According to that principle:

> *Totalism*: For any populations, α and β, α is, all else equal, better than β if and only if the total sum of (positive and negative) welfare at α is greater than at β.

The second argument is a more compelling development of the Totalism-based argument above. It entails the Repugnant Conclusion via a chain of steps each of which is described by the following principle:

> *Quantity*: For any populations, α and β, both of which consist of lives at positive, perfectly equal welfare-levels, if the welfare-level at β is only marginally lower than at α, then, if β has a sufficiently greater population than α, then, all else equal, β is better.

The third argument is rather different. In its most compelling form it proceeds by a series of steps described by the Dominance-Addition Principle and Non-Anti-Egalitarianism:

> *Dominance-Addition Principle*: For any populations, α and β, if α consists of lives at a positive, equal welfare-level, and β consists of the same number of lives, but at a higher welfare-level, plus some other lives at any positive welfare level, then β is, all else equal, better.

> *Non-Anti-Egalitarianism*: For any populations, α and β, both of which consist of positive-welfare lives, if β is more equal than α and contains both more total welfare and has a higher average welfare, then β is, all else equal, better.

Both the second and third arguments rely on some form of Transitivity, the simplest of which is:

> *Transitivity*: For any populations α, β, χ, if α is better than β and β is better than χ, then α is better than χ.

This allows us to derive the Repugnant Conclusion. If any of these three arguments is sound, then the Repugnant Conclusion is true.

Notes

1   There are more fine-grained distinctions in ordering than these (ordinal or cardinal) that I ignore here.

2 Parfit's initial (1984) derivation of the Repugnant Conclusion is based on a (weaker) variant of Totalism: '(V)', or 'the Impersonal Total Principle'. See also Parfit (2016). Some of those who accept the Repugnant Conclusion including Dasgupta (forthcoming), Tännsjö (2004) and Broome (2004) also rely on variants of this principle. I discuss some of these – including the variations amongst them – at greater length below.

3 For discussion of the significance (or lack thereof) of the evaluative/deontic distinction in dealing with problematic results in population axiology, see Arrhenius (2004).

4 For discussion of the varieties of ways – temporal and modal – in which one might apply a weighted form of person-affecting principle, see Arrhenius (2009).

5 One might think not given that it would seem to require attributing some level of goodness to one's *non-existence*; namely, a higher or lower level than one's existence (e.g. Dasgupta 1995, Broome 2004). For some potential ways around this, see Arrenhius and Rabinowicz (2017) and Holtug (2010).

6 See e.g., Temkin (1993). I am referring here to 'narrow' versions of the principle.

7 See especially Holtug (2004). For a contractualist approach to population ethics, see Finneron-Burns (2017).

8 For useful discussion, see e.g. List (2003), Greaves and Lederman (2016).

9 See Thomas (2017).

10 With this principle, as with all of the principles used in this book, there are many possible formulations. I have chosen formulations throughout with a view to optimising readability without, hopefully, compromising on detail that wold be significant for the aims of this book. I return to this at various junctures throughout with respect to specific principles.

11 An excellent sources that covers similar ground is Arrhenius and Tännsjö (2017).

12 Arrhenius (2000).

13 That we can do this, or what the constraints on doing it are, is subject of recent critical scrutiny, as noted in the fifth and sixth assumptions listed at the end of the previous section.

14 Classic variants on this are presented by Hurka (1983), Ng (1989) and Sider (1991).

15 This describes Hurka (1983).

16 This view is defended by e.g. Blackorby, Bossert and Donaldson (2004). A similar view is defended by Broome (2004). I discuss this at length in Chapter 4.

17 The use of views of this kind to respond to population paradoxes are discussed at length in Arrhenius (2005) and forthcoming.

18 Diagrams of this kind are a rough guide only for lexical priority views given that – amongst other things – they represent populations on either side of the threshold as separated by a finite distance.

19 It is questionable what this would be. This depends on the structure of welfare. See Thomas (2017).

20 A defender of the Lexical-Priority View would be likely to concede that this is an unsatisfactory result but argue that the unsatisfactoriness is merely a consequence of thinking that the cut-off need be *sharp*. If there can be *non-sharp* cut-offs, the problem outlined above does not arise. This is Parfit's (2016) preferred solution. He argues for a Lexical-Priority View with a non-sharp cut-off. Parfit articulates this in terms of a relation – the 'imprecisely better-than' relation that

holds between populations that are within the range of non-sharp cut-offs. He could equally have appealed to generic considerations regarding vagueness of value. See Dougherty (2014) for discussion. For a specific response that articulates why Parfit's preferred solution fails, see Arrhenius (2016).

21 See e.g. Parfit (2016: 116) for this label. An early presentation is Parfit (1984). See also Arrhenius (forthcoming) for precise variants on arguments of this kind.

22 Originally following Parfit (1984: 404). The formulation used here is similar to his 'principle (A)' (2016: 116). The now-canonical presentation of this is due to Gustaf Arrhenius (forthcoming).

23 Arrhenius (2003).

24 See e.g. Arrhenius (forthcoming). Arrenhius's formulations do differ from mine in some respects. I look at some of Arrhenius's formulations of principles used to derive the Repugnant Conclusion (though not Quantity specifically) in Chapter 4.

25 See e.g. Temkin (1987, 2012) and Chang (2016).

26 Relevant sources are Parfit (1984, 2016), Ng (1989) and especially Arrhenius (2001, 2011 and forthcoming).

27 The version presented here is closet to Ng (1989).

28 This version is closest to that in Huemer (2008) and Parfit (2016).

29 Although Huemer actually formulates it so that the population sizes are identical. A later, significantly weakened version of this principle in Chapter 4 includes this assumption.

30 See e.g. Arrhenius (2000, 2011 and forthcoming).

3   The Quality of Life Strategy

The Repugnant Conclusion is that:

> Compared with the existence of many people who would all have some
> very high quality of life, there is some much larger number of people
> whose existence would be better, even though these people would all
> have lives that are barely worth living.

Or, as I shall say for short: Z is better than A. In the previous chapter, three
arguments for this were presented. At least the second and third of these
arguments are reasonably compelling, the third especially so. What is
the upshot of this? Either there is a flaw in the reasoning that leads to the
Repugnant Conclusion, or it is true. I do not claim to rule out the former
option here, but my focus in this short monograph is on the latter. I am interested in whether the Repugnant Conclusion could, in fact, be true.

To see how one might go about arguing for this, take a step back. I noted
at the beginning of the first chapter that the arguments for the Repugnant
Conclusion are specific instances of a much more general kind of argument:
a paradox. A paradox is a seemingly sound argument with a conclusion that
seems clearly false. There are two strategies for resolving a paradox. One
is to show that one or more of the argument's premises are false or that it
is invalid. The other is to accept its soundness whilst 'explaining away'
the seeming falsity of the conclusion. This requires providing a *debunking*
argument: an explanation of *why* the conclusion seems clearly false that
is consistent with its actually being true. In moral philosophy, these kinds
of debunking arguments are not uncommon. The nineteenth-century moral
philosophers Marx and Nietzsche offered debunking arguments against
the moral norms that they encountered; arguments that explained away
the seeming truth of those norms in terms of their socially dubious origins. In contemporary moral philosophy, similar debunking arguments are

sometimes applied to some sub-class of ordinary moral intuitions on the basis of their evolutionary origins. The argument that we consider for the remainder of this chapter is, in a sense, similar. It too is a debunking argument. The idea is to explain why the Repugnant Conclusion is commonly thought to be repugnant in a sense that is consistent with its truth. If we can do so we will have resolved the paradox.

There are a number of different debunking arguments that one could reasonably use to respond to attempt to debunk the seeming repugnance of the Repugnant Conclusion. The option that we shall pursue is called *The Quality of Life Strategy*.[1] In this chapter, I set out the Quality of Life Strategy and explain its appeal. I defend it against common objections. In the next chapter, I explain why, despite this, it doesn't succeed.

3.1 The Quality of Life Strategy

According to the Quality of Life Strategy, we mistakenly think that the Repugnant Conclusion is clearly false because we have the wrong picture of what a life of marginally positive welfare, or simply 'life at Z', is like. We picture it as being much worse than it in fact is. That's why we think the Repugnant Conclusion must be false. But life at Z is much *better* than we picture it to be. Once we have an accurate picture of what life at Z is actually like, the Repugnant Conclusion no longer looks obviously false. It looks like a conclusion that could be true. Given this and given that we have compelling arguments for its truth, we should accept it.

To see why this is a promising approach recall what the Repugnant Conclusion states. It makes a comparative claim about two populations. One of those populations consists of a comparatively small number of lives at a comparatively high level of welfare. The second consists of a very much larger population of lives at a level of welfare that is only marginally positive. It is, one might think, essential to the seeming repugnance of the Repugnant Conclusion that the lives in the second population are – in terms of their welfare – marginally positive. It wouldn't seem repugnant if the welfare level of the larger population were much higher. The Quality of Life Strategy asks us to focus on this. According to defenders of the Quality of Life Strategy, we have the wrong idea of what life at Z is like. It is much better than we at first think. Once we realise this, the comparison between the two populations looks very different: the Repugnant Conclusion doesn't look repugnant any more at all. As I shall understand it, the Quality of Life Strategy consists of the following two claims:

> *A Surprising Claim*: A life of marginally positive welfare is not unlike the kinds of lives lived by privileged people today.

Paradox Resolution: When we recognise this, the Repugnant Conclusion no longer seems repugnant. Although it may still be counter-intuitive, it falls within the bounds of possibility such that – given that we already have powerful arguments for it – we should accept it.

A number of writers have defended this kind of approach. I shall begin by running through some examples: Partha Dasgupta, Clarke Wolf, Tobjorn Tännsjö and Jesper Ryberg. The reason for running through these four is twofold. Firstly, I want to give a sense of the widespread appeal of the view and the common core that these four writers share. Secondly, I want to highlight some differences of emphasis between them. These differences will be important when it comes to the objections to the Quality of Life Strategy that we will consider later in this chapter and again in Chapter 4.

Dasgupta

Partha Dasgupta has developed a complete population axiology that is a variant on Totalism. Suitably qualified, Dasgupta's view entails the Repugnant Conclusion. I shall briefly state some of the qualifications before explaining how Dasgupta makes use of the Quality of Life Strategy.[2]

The first important qualification is that Dasgupta's population axiology is dynamic: it is designed to deal with multiple generations. It is thus more sophisticated than the simple, single-generational model that I have presented to this point. On Dasgupta's model, the present generation should not weight the welfare of future generations equally to their own. Effectively, a discount factor applies to the welfares of future generations. Dasgupta's, then, is a 'generation relative' version of Totalism.[3] The second important qualification concerns the conditions under which Dasgupta take his view to entail the Repugnant Conclusion. Dasgupta distinguishes between actual-world scenarios and what he refers to as 'genesis' scenarios. In actual-world scenarios, we are concerned with what population it would be best to create given our present state. This will be determined by the size, growth rate and welfare of the current population as well as their preferences and the available resources. In genesis scenarios, we are concerned with what population it would be best to create *ex nihilo*: the population that, so to speak, *God* would create.

These are important variations that make Dasgupta's endorsement of the Repugnant Conclusion somewhat qualified. But there are some specific cases in which he does endorse it nonetheless, and his first line of defence is the Quality of Life Strategy. Central to this is the claim that Parfit and – writing earlier but in a similar vein – Henry Sidgwick mischaracterise what a marginally good life is like. They characterise it as significantly worse than it in fact is. Begin with Sidgwick. Writing a century before Parfit, Sidgwick was, it is commonly claimed, the first to recognise that Totalism entails the Repugnant Conclusion.[4] Dasgupta takes this as his departure point. He claims that Sidgwick's interpretation of the Repugnant Conclusion was mistaken. It was mistaken because Sidgwick had the wrong idea about what a marginally positive life is like. Sidgwick thought it as worse than it in fact is. This is because he mistakenly conceptualised a life at the neutral level as a life such that one would, throughout it, be neutral between suicide and continued existence. This is a mistake, Dasgupta claims, because a life that is neutral between suicide and continued existence is a life with *negative* welfare.[5] It follows that a life with marginally positive welfare must be significantly better than Sidgwick had thought. Dasgupta's basic reasoning for this (i.e. for thinking that suicidal life is worse than a life at the neutral level) is that there are many reasons that someone would choose not to commit suicide *despite* one's poor quality of life. In a striking passage, he writes:

> Religious prohibition, fear of the process of dying (the possibility of suffering pain, the feeling of isolation), the thought that one would be betraying family and friends, and the deep resistance to the idea of taking one's own life that has been built into us through selection pressure would cause someone even in deep misery to balk. It may even be that no matter what life throws at us we adjust to it, if only to make it possible to carry on.
>
> Dasgupta 2019: 62

From this, it follows that a life of marginally positive welfare must be significantly better than a suicidal life. Dasgupta identifies a similar error in Parfit's characterisation of the Repugnant Conclusion. Recall Parfit's initial characterisation (italics mine):

> For any possible population of at least ten billion people, all with a very high quality of life, there must be some much larger imaginable population whose existence, if other things are equal, would be better even though its members have *lives that are barely worth living*.

Here, Dasgupta thinks, Parfit has gone wrong: he too has misunderstood what life at the neutral level – and so a life of marginally positive welfare – is like. He has understood it as being much lower than it in fact is. Parfit characterises a life of marginally positive welfare as a life that is *barely worth living.* But this is a mischaracterisation. A life that is barely worth living – much like a life lived at neutrality between suicide and continued existence – is a *bad* life; a life of *negative* welfare. Dasgupta writes:

> Someone whose life is barely worth living doesn't enjoy a life of positive quality, she suffers from a life that is not only not good (as experienced by her), but is positively bad. In the contemporary world over a half billion people are malnourished and prone regularly to illness and disease, many of whom are also debt ridden, but who survive and tenaciously display that their lives are worth living by the fact that they persist in wishing to live.
>
> Dasgupta 2019: 63

Dasgupta's, I think plausible, idea is that there are many features of a life that make it worth living *despite* its low welfare level: perhaps, for example, the fulfilment of one's moral duties. The lesson again is that a life of minimally positive welfare is better than one might have thought. So how *should* we think of such a life? Dasgupta offers several different suggestions. The core idea is that rather than thinking about the neutral level in terms of one's preferences to continue to exist or cease to exist (as Sidgwick had done), we should think about it in terms of what kind of life we would comfortably *create*. Dasgupta writes:

> The acid test... is to ask ourselves whether we shouldn't pause before creating a person so as to imagine the kind of life that is likely to be in store for the potential child.
>
> Dasgupta 2019: 63

What is the consequence of this? Dasgutpa's thought is that the 'acid test' identified above should lead us to significantly raise our estimation of what a marginally positive quality of life is. There are many lives that we might reasonably hesitate to create in virtue of their welfare levels; lives that may be *far* better than that of the suicidal individual. This drives up (our conception of) the neutral level and so of the quality of a marginally positive life. Perhaps, it drives it up quite far:

> I have heard it said that [the neutral level] is the point of indifference between dying and continuing to live, or the point of indifference between life and death... [this] is misconceived. [This] also steers us away from... such figures as the World Bank's 1.90 dollars-a-day... [A] life of poverty represents a bad state of affairs for that individual,

and so makes the state of the world less good than it would otherwise be…. higher than the World Bank's poverty line.

Dasgupta 2019: 45

Dasgupta's thought is that the global poor lead bad lives; lives of negative welfare. It is only the privileged – those whose lives are not blighted by poverty and need – who lead lives of positive, even marginally positive, welfare. One might object. Isn't this conclusion in tension with Dasgupta's 'acid test' identified above? After all many billions of people (parents) bring others into existence (children) even though the resulting lives are below the kind of level that Dasgupta identifies? Doesn't this show that Dasgupta's acid test fails to deliver the result that he claims for it; namely, that a marginally positive welfare-level is at a higher level than the lives of the global poor? Dasgupta's response is structurally similar to that used to tackle both Sidgwick and Parfit. It is that these many billions of parents are motivated to bring children into existence *despite* the low welfare level of those children. One may choose to procreate, for example, because of the role that children play in the economy of one's household or because of the necessity of children to care for one in old age. This – the necessity of children in traditional developing-world households – is a prominent theme in much of Dasgupta's writing on development.[6]

With all of this in place, the Repugnant Conclusion should start to look significantly less repugnant than we might at first have thought. A minimally good life is better than we are likely to have thought. It is better than the lives of many billions of people alive today (or in the past).[7] It is more like a privileged life by today's standards. And so it becomes much *less* repugnant that a large number of lives lived *at this level* should be better than a much smaller number at a significantly higher level.

Wolf

There are many of Dasgupta's general axiological commitments that Clark Wolf does not share: whereas Dasgupta defends a 'generation relative' variation on classical utilitarianism, Wolf's view is a modified version of a *negative* utilitarianism. But Wolf's take on the Repugnant Conclusion is nonetheless very similar to Dasgupta's. He too defends an instance of what I have termed The Quality of Life Strategy.[8] His core claim is that:

[M]uch of the repugnance associated with the repugnant conclusion derives from the way in which marginally good lives have been characterised… [W]hen I consider the world of Parfit's repugnant conclusion to be inhabited by people... as I would have them... the repugnance has worn thin.

Wolf 2004: 76

Why does Wolf think this? Like Dasgupta, Wolf is resistant to Parfit's characterisation of a life of minimally positive welfare as a life 'barely worth living'. This phrase, he thinks, is misleading. The phrasing that he prefers is of a life that is 'just barely good'. So how should we characterise such a life? Wolf initially considers – and rejects – the following two proposals:

> Life is marginally above the neutral level at the point where one is indifferent between continuing to live and committing suicide.

> Life is marginally above the neutral level at the point where one is indifferent between continuing to live and present death.

Wolf rejects the first proposal: neutrality between continued life and suicide is not an appropriate measure. The reason for this is very similar to that offered by Dasgupta:

> People who are indifferent to suicide... are typically people who are miserable, suffering, and very badly off indeed.

Wolf 2004: 75

So lives that are indifferent to suicide are, Wolf thinks, lives with *negative* welfare. The same is true of the second proposal. This level too is, then, the level of someone who has a bad quality of life:

> People whose lives offer so little pleasure or fulfilment that they are indifferent to death are in a bad situation. Their lives are bad lives.

Wolf 2004: 76

So Wolf is claiming that the first two proposals are inaccurate characterisations of the neutral level and hence of a marginally positive quality of life. What is a better proposal? It is that an appropriate way of thinking about a marginally good quality of life is in terms of who we would be happy to *create*. Wolf provides the following specific proposal:

> Life is marginally above the neutral level just in case you knew that any child someone else conceived would enjoy at least that level of well-being, you would not regard that person as having a reason (deriving from consideration of the child's welfare) not to conceive a child.

Wolf, 2004: 77

This should be recognisable as a variant on Dasgupta's 'acid test': when thinking about neutral quality of life we should not focus on suicide or neutrality with respect to continued life. We should rather focus on what life we could comfortably *create*. And, also similarly to Dasgupta's view, in doing so we should set aside distorting factors owing to how the created life might influence our own prosperity – hence Wolf' reference to 'any child *someone else* may conceive'. So far so similar. What does Wolf think happens when we actually *apply* this proposal? What kinds of life should we end up identifying as lying at, or marginally above, the neutral level? Primarily, Wolf claims that applying it allows us to see that some possible characterisations of a marginally positive life are *wrong*. Consider the following proposal:

> Life is marginally above the neutral level if it is dull, uneventful, and ordinary. In such a life, nothing is pleasurable, though nothing is painful or undesirable either.

This, Wolf claims, is mistaken. Much like the first two proposals that he considered above it too under-estimates the quality of a marginally positive life. This life would not pass Wolf's variant on Dasgupta's 'acid test'. This is because, as Wolf simply puts it, a boring life is a bad life.[9] Wolf's thought, then, is that a marginally good life will look a lot better than we might initially have thought. It looks better than a life lived at indifference to suicide or death. It also looks better than a boring life. It looks good enough that it is no longer repugnant that enough of these lives could in fact be better than a small number of much higher quality lives.

To this point, Wolf's and Dasgupta's presentations are very similar. Both express sympathy for understanding a marginally good life in terms of the welfare level of someone that a reasonable and impartial person would consent to the creation of. I shall largely discuss Wolf under this description in the remainder of this chapter. I should note however – a point that I shall return to in Chapter 4 – that Wolf in fact goes on to defend a somewhat stronger proposal than that presented above. According to this stronger proposal, we should in fact use the truth of the Repugnant Conclusion itself as the bar by which to set a marginally good life. Such a life is, according to this proposal, simply that quality of life such that it is no longer repugnant that any number of these lives could be superior to a smaller number of lives of higher welfare (whatever that level). He proposes that:

> At some level of well-being, it is no longer repugnant to think of numerous people or even innumerable people living at that level, no longer odd to think that we might reasonably be indifferent between a world in which fewer people were even more blissful, and a more numerous

world in which people were only just so blissful. Life is marginally above the neutral level when it is at least as good as this.

Wolf 2004: 78

This is clearly a rather different direction from the 'acid test' sketched above. I am sceptical of whether it is a good way of conceptualising the quality of life at Z. I return to this, as I say, in Chapter 4 below.

Tännsjö

Torbjorn Tännsjö acknowledges that his classical utilitarian view entails the Repugnant Conclusion, but he does not thereby reject that view. Rather he employs the Quality of Life Strategy to defend it.[10] His use of the Quality of Life Strategy is prefigured by a more general methodological point. To describe the Repugnant Conclusion as 'repugnant' is, he claims, to describe it as *obviously false*. This is significant. It is familiar in moral philosophy that counter-intuitive conclusions can be true. We can be rational in accepting these conclusions if the arguments for them are sufficiently strong. But in labelling the Repugnant Conclusion as *repugnant* Parfit – and others who reject it – are claiming that it is not a conclusion of this form. It is a conclusion that is sufficiently far off-centre that it is not a candidate for rational acceptance, no matter how strong the arguments for it.[11]

Bearing this in mind, Tännsjö understands his task as follows: provide an argument for the view that the Repugnant Conclusion is not in fact *repugnant* – an argument for the view that the Repugnant Conclusion is a candidate for being just another counter-intuitive truth. The Quality of Life Strategy is one part of this. Tännsjö's basic presentation of the strategy is again similar to Dasgupta's and Wolf's. He too thinks that the seeming repugnancy of the Repugnant Conclusion is, in part at least, a consequence of mischaracterisation of what a life of minimally positive welfare – 'life at Z' – is like. It is based on the view that:

> [A]n enormous population of lives just worth living would look something like a vast concentration camp. I believe this to be a mistake... [m]any people probably live lives that are... not worth living. When this is acknowledged, the repugnant conclusion does not seem repugnant any more.
>
> Tännsjö 2004: 223

Why is this? At least one of Tännsjö's arguments is recognisably similar to those that we have seen in the work of Dasgupta and Wolf. It is that we should not think about minimally positive welfare in terms of suicide. Here,

Tännsjö agrees that there are many reasons that someone may forbear from suicide although their lives are, in terms of their welfare, bad. Beyond this, however, Tännsjö's arguments diverge somewhat from those of Dasgupta and Wolf. The divergence primarily concerns Tännsjö's focus on the ills of even privileged lives. These lives are not, he argues, all that we might ordinarily take them to be. This is well-illustrated by Tännsjö's approving quotation of an earlier variant of the Quality of Life Strategy that he attributes to Mackie. According to this view:

> [A] level that is marginally better than non-existence must already constitute a high degree of flourishing, and beyond this little further improvement is possible.
>
> Tännsjö 2004: 223

Tännsjö endorses a similar view; a view according to which the quality of human life rarely – if ever – rises far above the neutral level. The neutral level is, then, the level that describes not just *good* lives but some of the *best* lives with which we are familiar. In a striking passage, Tännsjö outlines, in terms that he acknowledges to be somewhat impressionistic, his reasons for thinking this.

> [N]o matter how 'lucky' we are, how many gadgets we possess, we rarely reach beyond this level... Most of the time we spend waiting for all kinds of things and events. We often wait in vain. And when Godot arrives, if eventually he does, he isn't always such a great acquaintance to make... many of the good things in life come with a price tag to be paid in terms of suffering.
>
> Tännsjö 2004: 223

This marks a difference of emphasis between Tännsjö's argument and those of Dasgupta and Wolf. Tännsjö seems to be arguing that our own lives are worse than we take them to be. We over-rate their quality.[12] This pessimism about how we rate our own lives is no part of Dasgupta's case or of Wolf's. It is clearer still in some of Tännsjö's additional arguments. I discuss these in more detail, and so fill out Tännsjö's view – and what it means for the Quality of Life Strategy – later in this chapter.

Ryberg

The final example is Jesper Ryberg.[13] Much like Dasgupta, Wolf and Tännsjö, Ryberg rejects the identification of a minimally good life with a life lived at the point of suicide. He does so for much the same reason:

factors other than one's welfare can cause one's decision to continue one's life. This can, and does, lead many people to persist in living *despite* their welfare living. He writes:

> Many people probably have a disposition to cling to life even under the most terrible conditions.
>
> Ryberg 2004: 244

Ryberg provides a further argument for this claim. One interesting argument is that there is a well-known connection between misery and a lack of initiative. What Ryberg means by this, I take it, is that depression is often accompanied by – or perhaps is partly *constituted* by – a certain kind of weakness of will: the failure to act rationally, including, presumably, the failure to act in ways that one knows to be good for one. This negative characterisation – concerning how life worth living should *not* be understood – is coupled with a further negative characterisation that is recognisably similar to Dasgupta's. It is that many people alive today – the identities of whom overlap significantly with those to whom we saw Dasgupta referring earlier – lead lives that are actually bad (in terms of welfare)

> People whose lives are a struggle for survival, who live with the permanent fear of being killed or losing relatives, or who are racked by depressions or anxiety, belong to this category. Such lives are properly described as crimped and mean and the tragedy is that there are millions of such lives.
>
> Ryberg 2004: 242

These are lives of negative welfare. Life at Z is better than this. But how, *positively*, does Ryberg think a life worth living should be characterised? Here he is cautious but the basic idea is that lives worth living may look like the lives of relatively privileged people. Rather like Tännsjö, Ryberg's case for this positive claim is coupled with a rather pessimistic picture of what the best human lives are actually like. They are, he thinks, worse than we might ordinarily think; we tend to over-rate their goodness. His thought, to paraphrase, is that the case for thinking that life at Z is like an ordinary privileged life is based as much on a pessimistic picture of a privileged life as on a negative picture of the life of, for example, the global poor. What is the reasoning behind this pessimistic impression? Ryberg's picture of an 'ordinary, privileged' life is of one that is characterised largely by 'neutral' experiences, experiences that are neither good nor bad: sleeping, passing the time, sitting in the office and so on. Beyond this, experiences tend not to rise or fall much below the neutral level. And of those that do, they distribute roughly equally above and below the neutral level. As Ryberg puts it:

> A more apposite picture... contains several periods at neutrality... the time we spend sleeping [and] periods which, though they are not at all unhappy, do not make our lives any better... Moreover a life also contains a number of happy experiences and unhappy experiences, but it is not the case that the former vastly outweigh the latter; neither when it comes to the minor deflections in our daily life, but nor the more steep fluctuations which now and then – relatively rarely, I suggest – befall us.
>
> Ryberg 2004: 242

In this passage Ryberg's emphasis looks rather closer to that of Tännsjö than that of Dasgupta and Wolf. Like Tännsjö, Ryberg is most readily understood as emphasising that lives like ours are surprisingly bad or at least worse than we might have thought: they contain a lot of 'neutrality' and an even split of positive and negative experiences. I shall return to this later in the chapter. I shall also return to some of Ryberg's additional arguments; notably his appeal to the existence of psychological mechanisms that lead to overly-optimistic self-assessment of one's quality of life in establishing his pessimistic claims.

3.2 Formulating the Quality of Life Strategy

I have briefly sketched four different examples of the use of the Quality of Life Strategy. Although these examples share some common ground, they also differ in important ways. Given that the aim of this book is to properly assess this strategy it is important to formulate it properly. We have already seen that the core claims are as follows:

> *Surprising Claim*: A life of marginally positive welfare is not unlike the kinds of lives lived by privileged people today.
>
> *Paradox Resolution*: When we recognise this, the Repugnant Conclusion no longer seems repugnant. Although it may still be counter-intuitive, it falls within the bounds of possibility such that – given that we already have powerful arguments for it – we should accept it.

Within this, a number of more specific claims have also been made some of which are common to all four, some of which are not. Perhaps the most obvious is:

Not Like Suicide: Life at Z is better than a life lived at neutrality between continued existence and suicide.

This claim was made by all defenders of the Quality of Life Strategy. Furthermore, the basic argument given for it seems like a good one. There are reasons that people would refrain from committing suicide *despite* their low welfare level. Given this, we should think of life lived at neutrality between continued existence and suicide as a *bad* life. *Not Like Suicide* seems to be both sensible and to represent common ground amongst the defenders of the Quality of Life Strategy.

Is there any more sensible, shared content to add to the Quality of Life Strategy? The obvious candidate is a claim made by both Dasgupta and Wolf concerning the positive characterisation of life at Z. It is that:

> *The Creation Test*: Life at Z is better than a life at which one would reasonably decide not to create someone in virtue of their quality of life.

This may look pretty well indisputable. Surely, one could reasonably choose to create a life when thinking only about its welfare only if that life were good, or had positive welfare. As I read them, however, Dasgupta and Wolf are really using the Creation Test as a staging-post to a stronger claim. It is that once we *use* it, we should revise our estimates of what life at Z is like *upwards*: it should show that life at Z is better than we might initially have thought. I am not so sure that they are right about this. One reason for scepticism is that even amongst defenders of the Quality of Life Strategy, there is bound to be significant latitude regarding what the Creation Test will tell us. Consider, for example, Clark Wolf's claim – encountered above – that if we accept the Creation Test, then we should reject the following:

> Life is marginally above the neutral level if it is dull, uneventful, and ordinary. In such a life, nothing is pleasurable, though nothing is painful or undesirable either.

I don't find this obvious. Consider Ryberg's characterisation of an ordinary privileged life again. He characterises it as being largely lived at 'neutrality', highlighting periods of sleep and disinterest, with positive and negative fluctuations being both less frequent than we might think, and largely evenly matched. This sounds very much like the 'boring' life that Wolf claims fails to pass the Creation Test ('dull, uneventful and ordinary'). But of course Ryberg claims that this kind of life *is* marginally above the neutral level. So there is quite a lot of room for manoeuvre here: it is far from clear whether the acceptance of the Creation Test really would drive up estimates of what life at Z is like in the way that Wolf (and I think Dasgupta) seem to think.

The second reason for scepticism is more general and more troubling. We should be at least somewhat sceptical of whether we can really use the Creation Test to make *any* estimates about quality of life, let alone to drive those estimates *up*. Suppose that I ask myself whether it would be reasonable to create someone, when thinking only about their welfare level. How would I go about answering this question? My natural reaction would be to ask whether the potential person's life would, in terms of its welfare, be net good or bad. It is only if their welfare would be net good that I would judge it reasonable to create them. Clearly, though, this would render the Creation Test redundant: if I knew whether a potential person's life were net good or bad, then I wouldn't need to think about whether it would be reasonable to create them in order to work this out (nor presumably should I). So if the Creation Test is to avoid redundancy, then its application must not require one to first ask oneself whether the potential person's life would, in terms of its welfare, be net good or bad. So how, then, *would* one work out whether, for a given life, it was reasonable to create it when thinking only about its welfare level? I confess that I am at a loss. I don't have access to a realm of facts about the reasonability of creating a life given its welfare level that is prior to the facts, whatever they may be, about the quality of that life. So I find it difficult to see how the Creation Test can do *any* work.

To this point I have addressed two claims that one may wish to incorporate within a general formulation of the Quality of Life Strategy: Not Like Suicide and the Creation Test. Consider a third claim, defended by both Dasgupta and Wolf, but not by either Tännsjö or Ryberg:

> *Against 'Not Worth Living'*: The use of the expression 'a life barely worth living' leads to underestimating the quality of life at Z.

Dasgupta argued that by characterising life at Z as barely worth living Parfit was inaccurately characterising those lives. He claimed that many people who have *bad* lives nonetheless have lives that are worth living. Should we agree with Dasgupta and accept Against 'Not Worth Living' as part of the characterisation of the Quality of Life Strategy? Broadly speaking, I think we should. We must be careful though.

It is helpful to begin by distinguishing between two senses of 'life barely worth living': a sense that pertains purely to welfare, and an all-things-considered sense. A life is barely worth living in a sense that pertains solely to welfare if it is a good life *with respect to and only to, welfare*. All lives at Z are, by definition, of this form. A life is barely worth living in an all-things-considered sense, by contrast, if it is worth living for reasons that are not restricted to the welfare of that person. They could include the role of that life with respect to dependents. Perhaps, for example, someone may have an all-things-considered life worth living if they play the morally important role of supporting their ailing parents, even though their own life is, in terms of welfare, bad. Or perhaps a troubled genius may leave a great artistic legacy and therefore have a life worth living, though in terms of welfare their life was terrible.

With this distinction in place, we can be more precise in our scepticism about Parfit's characterisation of life at Z as barely worth living. 'Life worth living' is, I think, most naturally used in reference to the all-things-considered conception. But so understood, it is likely false that life at Z is barely worth living. Lives at Z may be *well* worth living in the all-things-considered sense. This would be the case if, for example, ordinary lives gain much of their 'worth-livingness' from their moral properties. And so Dasgupta may well be right as against Parfit. This is of course compatible with the claim that if we restrict ourselves to the strictly welfare-based sense of 'life worth living', then Parfit is right to characterise life at Z in this way. But so restricted, the Repugnant Conclusion does not sound as obviously alarming. It *is* obviously alarming that an enormous number of lives that are barely worth living *in the all-things-considered sense* might be better than a small number of wonderful lives. This is because of how bad such lives are; these are lives that are devoid not only of welfare but also of moral or aesthetic significance. But it is less obviously alarming that an enormous number of lives that are barely worth living *in the welfare-restricted sense* might be better than a small number of wonderful lives. As a result, I think we should agree with Dasgupta and accept a properly specified version of Against 'Not Worth Living' as part of the Quality of Life Strategy.

This completes the initial presentation of the Quality of Life Strategy. I should note that I have passed over two important points. The first is the contrast in emphasis between the presentations of Dasgupta and Wolf on the one hand, and Tännsjö and Ryberg on the other; a point that I flagged briefly earlier. I return to this in more detail later in this chapter. Here I discuss, amongst other things, Tännsjö's views about the possibility of a limit to how good an ordinary human life can be. The second important point that I have passed over concerns the idea – expressed by Wolf above – that we should use the truth of the Repugnant Conclusion itself in order to set the quality of a marginally good life. I return to this in the context of discussing John Broome's views in Chapter 4. For now, we move on to consider some complexities that concern how we should understand 'the neutral level'.

3.3 Further issues with quality of life

To this point the discussion of quality of life – and specifically of a marginally positive quality of life – has been highly abstract. There has been little discussion of how we should understand quality of life – and specifically of a marginally positive quality of life – in more concrete terms, or of the many ways that marginally positive qualities of life can vary. We need to think about this. A good place to start is with a very simple picture of how we should understand quality of life and of marginally positive quality of life specifically. We can then add complexity to this basic model and thereby examine how, if at all, it impacts on the feasibility of the Quality of Life Strategy.

Conceptually, the most straightforward way of thinking about quality of life is simple hedonism.[14] So understood the quality of a life is determined entirely by the quality of the hedonic states that it contains. These states can be either good ('pleasures') or bad ('pains') and can differ in both duration and intensity. The greater the duration or intensity (or some function of both) of a good state, the better. The greater the duration or intensity (or some function of both) of a bad state, the worse. This allows for a simple way of thinking about quality of life and therefore of marginally positive quality of life. On this model, a good life just is a life that contains a surplus of the good over the bad, and a bad life is just a life that contains a surplus of the bad over the good. A marginally good life is a life in which the surplus of the good over the bad is marginal. A neutral life is a life at which the goods and the bads are perfectly balanced, or in which there are no goods or bads at all.

We can use this simple model to approach the Quality of Life Strategy. It states that ordinary privileged lives contain a marginal surplus of the good hedonic states over the bad and that lives at Z are like this. Lives at higher-average welfare worlds, like A, are simply lives that have a greater surplus. This simple model fits reasonably well with some of the defences of the Quality of Life Strategy sketched above. There are however different (i.e. non-hedonic) models and even within the simple hedonic model there are significant variations in what marginally positive lives can look like. I touch briefly on four such models and variations below. This is important as they may affect the tenability of the Quality of Life Strategy: perhaps, for example, that strategy only looks plausible – or looks most plausible – if we adopt the kind of relatively simple hedonic model above, or some minor variant on it.

The shape of a life

Different lives have different 'shapes'. A 'flat' life is a life lived at a fairly constant quality throughout. A 'rollercoaster' life, by contrast, is lived at very different quality levels across its duration, including some 'peaks' and some 'troughs'. These lives have very different shapes. A further alternative is a life lived at a non-zero, but fairly constant gradient: a life that either steadily improves or worsens from beginning to end. Simple hedonists would, in principle, rank all of these lives equally provided that they contain the same overall surplus of good states over bad, or bad over good. It is not obvious however that this tracks our ordinary appraisal. One might think for example that lives with positive gradients are better than lives with negative gradients.[15]

Lives at Z could, in principle, have any number of these different shapes. Could this affect the plausibility of the Quality of Life Strategy? It isn't obvious how it would. Reflection on the significance of the shape of a life for assessing overall quality of life might lead us to reject hedonism. This is because hedonism does not account for the variation in the quality of lives of different shapes well. But it is not obvious that it would *thereby* cause us to reject the Quality of Life Strategy. We would simply need to understand what life at Z is like in non-hedonic terms (or in *non-simple* hedonic terms). But the basic Quality of Life Strategy would remain intact. Or more precisely, it would remain intact unless only simple hedonic views deliver the intuitions that defenders of the Quality of Life Strategy need (namely, that life at Z is a bit like an ordinary privileged life). But that would require a separate argument. We turn to this below.

Non-hedonic measures

Suppose then that an alternative, non-hedonic view is correct. There are two obvious options: desire-satisfaction views and objective-list views. According to desire-satisfaction views, one's welfare is a matter of the satisfaction of one's desires so that: one's life goes well to the extent that one's desires – or perhaps some idealisation of one's desires – are satisfied, and badly to the extent that one's desires are not satisfied. According to objective-list views, one's welfare is a matter of the presence of certain goods within. These goods are commonly thought to include, for example, meaning, meaningful relationships and certain types of success or achievement. One's life goes well to the extent that it possesses them. One's life goes badly to the extent that – depending on the details of the view – it either lacks these goods, or possesses some 'bads' which could include depression, loneliness and failure.[16]

Would the truth of either of these views – as opposed to the hedonic view – undermine the case for the Quality of Life Strategy? I don't see any reason to think that they would. The basic structure of the Quality of Life Strategy would remain unchanged. The structure is that the marginally positive lives at Z are like our own and that the Repugnant Conclusion is therefore no-longer repugnant. Furthermore, the plausibility of this basic point – that the marginally positive lives at Z are like our own – seems largely unaffected by switching from hedonic to desire-satisfaction or objective-list views of welfare. All that is necessary is to show that lives like ours possess a marginal surplus of the goods over the bads. It is not difficult to see how the basic arguments would transfer.

We can construct the same kind of 'impressionistic' case given by defenders of the Quality of Life Strategy whether we understand welfare in terms of hedonic states, desire-satisfaction or an objective-list. The quotations given above from Dasgupta, Wolf, Tännsjö and Ryberg can in fact be read in any of these spirits. The bads that they identify as besetting many lives include, for example, the fear of being killed or losing relatives, being racked with depression and anxiety, and being malnourished and prone to disease. These could easily feed into the impressionistic case in favour of the Quality of Life Strategy whether we think of welfare in terms of hedonic states, desire-satisfaction or an objective-list.

My claim here, to be clear, is that it is not hard to create the same 'impressionistic' view of the quality of human life that informs the Quality of Life Strategy whether we work with hedonic theories of welfare or some alternative. It is, then, plausible that the following conditional holds: If defenders of the Quality of Life Strategy are right that quality of life understood in hedonic terms yields the result that life at Z is a bit like an ordinary privileged life, then they would also be right to think that quality of life understood in terms of desire-satisfaction or objective-lists yields the result that life at Z is a bit like an ordinary privileged life too. This basic argument will be significantly strengthened below when we discuss the case for thinking that there are systematic reasons that we tend to over-estimate the quality of our lives: reasons that apply to any theory of welfare.

Quality or 'the best things in life'

As I have characterised it, life at Z is of marginally positive welfare and life at A is of high welfare. But one might worry that this characterisation leaves out an important part of what the Repugnant Conclusion really claims. As Parfit presents it, lives at Z and lives at A are contrasted, in part at least, by the *kinds* of goods that they contain. He imagines lives at Z to be drab, devoid of the best things in life, consisting of 'muzak and potatoes'.[17] Lives at A by contrast contain the best things in life (whatever these may be). When we characterise lives at A and Z, respectively in these ways, the Quality of Life Strategy is challenged. Can an enormous number of lives of muzak and potatoes really be better than a life that contains the very best things?

We must be careful here. Lives at Z need not contain only muzak and potatoes. They could be 'rollercoaster lives': lives that contain both the very worst things and the very best, but in balance.[18] Nor is it obvious that lives at A must contain the very best things: depending on one's view of welfare, they could just contain huge amounts of muzak and potatoes. Taking care over this point probably won't help though. The Repugnant Conclusion would be a threat provided that there is *some* characterisation of life at Z that contains only muzak and potatoes, and *some* characterisation of life at A that contains the very best things in life. Provided this is the case, it will still be the case (if the Repugnant Conclusion is true) that there is some enormous population of muzak-and-potatoes lives that is better than a small population of lives that contain the very best things. This is enough to generate the basic worry.

There are a number of different responses to this on behalf of a defender of the Quality of Life Strategy. The first response is that lives of muzak and potatoes are probably not good lives. They are probably bad lives. This kind of response is most obviously available to the defence of the Quality of Life Strategy as we find it in Wolf and Dasgupta. Recall that according to Wolf the following is false:

> Life is marginally above the neutral level if it is dull, uneventful, and ordinary.

It is false, he claims, because it over-estimates what life marginally above the neutral level is like. Yet it sounds very much like a life of 'muzak and potatoes'. So a life of muzak and potatoes turns out to be a bad life, not a good one. This arguably receives some independent support from some prominent 'objective list' theories of welfare. Consider, for example, the plausible view that objective bads include boredom, dullness or a lack of meaning.[19] This provides another route to the conclusion that a life of muzak and potatoes is a bad life, not a good life.

The second response is more obviously available to the defence of the Quality of Life Strategy as we find it in Tännsjö and Ryberg. It is that our own lives may not be so different from lives of muzak and potatoes after all. Recall Ryberg's characterisation of an ordinary privileged life as a life that is lived for long periods at neutrality and that rises steeply above or below this only occasionally (and then, in rough balance). That isn't entirely dis-similar to a life of muzak and potatoes. But now if we think that it isn't repugnant that an enormous number of ordinary privileged lives might be better than a small number of great lives, then we shouldn't think that it is repugnant that an enormous number of muzak-and-potatoes lives might be better than a small number of great lives either.

Either of these two options are available to a defender of the Quality of Life Strategy, depending on the nature of their initial defence of the view. Both are somewhat effective. Interestingly though, both pull in very different directions. I return to this in 2.5 below when discussing the difference in emphasis between the approach of Dasgupta and Wolf on one hand and Tännsjö and Ryberg on the other.

Peculiar lives, non-human lives

When presenting their view, defenders of the Quality of Life Strategy primarily discuss recognisably human lives. They discuss what, in ordinary human terms, life at Z would look like. Perhaps though, this is insufficient. We can conceive of *non-human* lives that fulfil the conditions for life at Z in strange ways. This could pose a problem for the Quality of Life Strategy.[20] Imagine a life in which a creature exists for billions of years, experiencing only a split second of happiness – and no unhappiness – in that time. This would – at least on the hedonic view – be a life at marginally positive welfare. So it would be a life at Z, albeit not a recognisably human one. Can we really accept that an enormous number of lives *like this* would be better than a small number of wonderful lives? It is not obvious that we can. This is a serious challenge to the Quality of Life Strategy.

One could, of course, use this as a basis to reject simple hedonism. But let's just set this to one side: when we are dealing with very peculiar lives we will, most likely, be able to construct a troubling example case *whatever* our theory of welfare. We need a more general response. One is that these are not the kinds of case that we should lean on when determining whether to accept or reject the Repugnant Conclusion. We are familiar with human lives and are at least somewhat comfortable with evaluating them. We are not similarly familiar with evaluating a life in which a creature exists for billions of years, experiencing only a split second of happiness (let alone populations comprised of enormous numbers of them). So we should not set any – or least not much – store by intuitive judgments about the value of these populations. This is Tännsjö's line:

> When considering a life such as this one I must admit that I feel not only that common sense morality fails us but also that my own moral intuition falters.
>
> Tännsjö, 2004: 229

We can understand Tännsjö as appealing to a principle. The principle is roughly the following:

Realism Constraint: When assessing the Repugnant Conclusion we should think about the nature and the quality of the lives of those who comprise the populations in familiar ways; our focus should be on recognisably human lives. These are the kinds of case on which our judgment is sufficiently robust.

There is surely some truth to this. Judgments about the comparative quality of life of different kinds of creature that are extremely different to ourselves are hardly the surest of foundations for axiological theorising. Nevertheless though, we need to be careful with this kind of principle. It is too easy to use it to (illegitimately) dismiss sensible challenges to the Quality of Life Strategy. Troublingly though, it is questionable whether pressuring the Quality of Life Strategy requires referring to such peculiar lives. It can be pressured with reference only to recognisable but non-standard human lives or to non-human lives, thereby rendering the Realism Constraint somewhat redundant.

Consider, for example, the lives of human beings with severe congenital mental impairments. It is surely conceivable – even if we accept the basic claims of the Quality of Life Strategy – that these humans should have lives of positive welfare, though their lives do not contain the goods enjoyed by human adults of typical development. The Repugnant Conclusion implies that a population consisting of a sufficient number of these lives is superior to a much smaller population of lives of adults of typical development. Doing so does not obviously violate the Realism Constraint. Or, to take a very different case, consider the lives of familiar household animals, for example dogs. Dogs can presumably have a good quality of life (I recall a former student saying that she would like to be a dog in a middle-class household because it seemed such a nice life). Although this would violate the Realism Constraint's focus on human life, it isn't obvious that this is a legitimate reason not to consider these lives. After all, we are reasonably familiar with them: although I wouldn't quite endorse my student's claim, I do suspect that my judgment of whether a dog is enjoying a good life is comparable in its reliability to my judgment of whether a human baby is enjoying a good life.

It seems then that a defender of the Quality of Life Strategy shouldn't lean too heavily on the Realism Constraint and that some bullets may yet have to be bitten. The hope for a defender of the Quality of Life Strategy is that for those cases that can't legitimately be dealt with by the Realism Constraint, it will be possible to either bite the bullet without its being repugnant to do so (though it may be counter-intuitive), or to provide some alternative explanation of why those cases are not genuine instances of the Repugnant

Conclusion; for example, perhaps the reason that a large population of dogs is not better than a smaller population of happy humans is that it illegitimately presupposes the possibility of interspecies welfare comparisons, or perhaps the implausibility of large, happy populations of those who suffer from severe mental disabilities only becomes apparent when we think dynamically – those populations may be unable to sustain the institutions necessary for their long-term or even inter-generational functioning.[21] It is not obvious to me whether or not this is in fact the case. I will be charitable at this point: I will assume that the Quality of Life Strategy is not fatally undermined by these kinds of case (though I return to some of these issues below).

Preview of forthcoming objections

The Quality of Life Strategy has now been outlined and some of the complexities in its characterisation have been noted. In the remainder of this chapter, several preliminary objections are presented. The aim of presenting these is to help to help to clarify the Quality of Life Strategy and – with respect to the first of the objections – to actually bring out its appeal. I address two more worrying objections in the final chapter: it is these rather than the objections in this chapter that will ultimately prove to be the downfall of the Quality of Life Strategy.[22]

3.4 Trading-off

Consider the following objection to the Quality of Life Strategy:[23]

> What is really repugnant about the superiority of Z over A is that Z *trades off* quality of life for quantity of lives. The Quality of Life Strategy doesn't address this at all. So it doesn't address what makes the Repugnant Conclusion repugnant. So it doesn't succeed.

This could make for a powerful objection to the Quality of Life Strategy. But in order to assess it, we must first interpret it. Specifically, we need to interpret the claim that what is really repugnant about the superiority of Z over A is that Z trades off quality of life for quantity of lives. On the most straightforward interpretation, this means:

> *Simple Trade-Off*: For any perfectly equal populations, α and β, if β has lower average welfare than α.

Clearly though, this can't be right. It is plausible that sometimes trading-off of quality for quantity *can* actually make a population better (or at least not worse). This is actually built in to some derivations of the Repugnant Conclusion. Consider again the second 'continuum-based' derivation offered in Chapter 2, represented by the following diagram (Figure 3.1):

The idea behind this derivation is that each individual step (e.g. A to B, B to C, C to D) improves or at least doesn't worsen the population (though all the steps together do worsen it). Yet each individual step represents just the kind of trade-off of quality for quantity that, if Simple Trade-Off is true, is repugnant. Note furthermore that we can make this basic point in much weaker – and so less contestable – terms. In order to reject Simple Trade-Off, we don't need to rely on the claim that, in Continuum Reasoning, each individual step improves or doesn't worsen the population. We need only rely on the much weaker claim that it isn't *repugnant* that each individual step (e.g. A to B, B to C, C to D) doesn't worsen the population. And we are surely entitled to this assumption. It would be absurd to claim that the superiority of B over A is *repugnant*.

So if the trade-off objection that we are considering is to be worth taking seriously it must be based on a weaker claim than Simple Trade-Off. One option would be that *large* trade-offs are repugnant:

> *Weaker Trade-Off*: For any perfectly equal populations, α and β, if β has a significantly lower average welfare than α, then, even if β is a much larger population than α, it is repugnant that β is better than α.

This is more plausible. It doesn't entail, implausibly, that it is repugnant that, in the Continuum Reasoning above, B is better than A. It merely implies that it is repugnant that A is worse than some population much further down the continuum such as M or N. Although this is more plausible, we should still worry that it is too strong. It is not obvious that M is worse than A and it is certainly not obvious that it is repugnant that M is better than A. Nor, to the best of my knowledge, is it commonly claimed otherwise. While it is typically thought that it is repugnant that Z is better than A, it is not typically

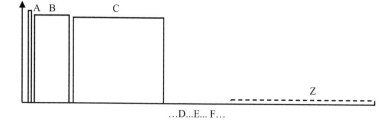

Figure 3.1

claimed that it is repugnant that M is better than A. This is not, I think, a mere contingency of the presentation of the Repugnant Conclusion. The conclusion that M is better than A could at most be somewhat surprising. The burden of proof would certainly be on someone who claims that it is repugnant.

This can be easily fixed. We need only modify Weaker Trade-Off to the claim that it is repugnant to trade-off quality for quantity *where the trade-off is the size of that between A and Z (or more)*. The result would be:

Weakest Trade-Off: For any perfectly equal populations, α and β, if β has an average welfare-level that is lower than that of α by at least the same amount that the average welfare-level at Z is lower than that at A, as A and Z figure in the Repugnant Conclusion, then, even if β is a much larger population than α, it is repugnant that β is better than α.

This is weaker than either of the previous two proposals. So it is in a sense more plausible. Is it plausible enough to show that the *real* problem with the Repugnant Conclusion is that it trades off quality for quantity and so that the Quality of Life Strategy fails? I don't think so. There is one initial problem, which is that it is peculiar to think that 'A' in the Repugnant Conclusion picks out some specific welfare-level: 'quality of life at A' could refer to a range of different welfare levels, much as populations size of Z could vary. But let's set this to one side. Suppose that 'quality of life at A' picks out some specific very high level of welfare and assign a value, v, to the difference in quality of life between that welfare level and the welfare level at Z. Now imagine that the continuum from A to Z is only the lower part of a much larger continuum, which extends beyond A to a range of lower number, higher average-welfare populations A_1, A_2, A_3 and so on. At some point, we will reach a population such that the welfare level at it is v higher than A. Let's call this population A_N. We can represent it as follows (Figure 3.2):

If Weakest Trade-Off is true, then it is repugnant that A is better than A_N. In fact, it is repugnant in exactly the same way that it is repugnant that Z is better than A. It is repugnant because the difference in welfare level between A and A_N is exactly that same as that between A and Z (namely, v). So we must now ask, is it repugnant that A is better than A_N? I don't think it is. A_N is a population in which an extremely small number of people (maybe one or two) lead incredibly wonderful lives. A is (say) a population in which a million people lead very good quality lives. I have no strong intuitions as regards which of these is better and I certainly don't think it so obvious that A_N is better than A that it would be *repugnant* should this be false.

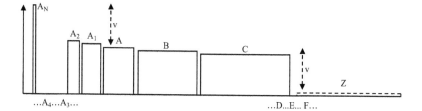

Figure 3.2

What is the lesson that we should learn from this? There are two lessons that go hand-in-hand. The first is that the trade-off objection isn't obviously sound. This is supported by the failure of the three interpretations of it provided above. The second more important lesson is that the basic move underlying the Quality of Life Strategy is a sensible one. We know that the supposed repugnance of Z's superiority over A isn't solely a result of the trade-off of quality for quantity. This as shown by the rejection of Simple Trade-Off. We also know that it isn't the *exact amount* of trade-off. This was shown by the rejection of Weaker Trade-Off and Weakest Trade-Off. So what is the source of the repugnance? The obvious answer is that it is trading off a high quality of life *for a quality of life that is merely marginally good*. The problem is with the superiority *of Z-like lives* over A-like lives. Why would this lend support to the Quality of Life Strategy? The Quality of Life Strategy is premised on the view that if quality of life at Z was better than we initially thought, we wouldn't find it repugnant that Z is better than A. This is what we would expect if the source of the repugnance were in large part a consequence of the unpleasant nature of life at Z. And that is precisely what the rejection of the three trade-off principles seems to show.

One way to bring this out is by comparison with the insight of *sufficientarian* views in political philosophy. Sufficientarians are a kind of egalitarian: they believe that there is something bad about unequal distributions of welfare.[24] What is distinctive of sufficientarians is that they believe unequal distributions are bad only where those involved have welfare levels that fall below a certain threshold. To take (a modification of) Roger Crisp's well-known example, while sufficientarians may believe that there is something bad about a distribution of welfare in which some people are super-rich and some are very poor, they don't believe there is something similarly bad about a distribution in which everyone is extremely well-off, but some are forced to drink a lower quality of fine wine than the other (Lafite 1982 versus Latour 1982).[25] At a sufficient level of generality there is, I think, a common spirit behind the sufficientarian thought and the claim (above) that it is not intuitively repugnant that A_N is better than A in anything like the way that it is when comparing A with Z. We should not expect comparisons between populations to behave in the same way at low welfare levels as at sufficiently high welfare levels. A significant difference in quality of life at low welfare levels may be bad in a way that an identical difference at higher levels is not – or at least not obviously so. Of course, this should not be over-interpreted. I am not claiming that the repugnance of the repugnant conclusion is *solely* a consequence of the nature of life at Z such that any trade-off that leads to Z-like lives is repugnant. If so, then it would be repugnant that, for example, Z is better than X. The fact that the trade-off is *from A to Z* is part of the picture. But the nature of life at Z is nonetheless clearly significant in a way that should lend support to a defender of the Quality of Life Strategy. By showing that what is seemingly problematic about the superiority of Z over A is largely dependent on the specific nature of Z and the trade-off to a population of lives *of this quality*, we should gain some degree of optimism that the Quality of Life Strategy is well-placed to make the Repugnant Conclusion seem less repugnant. This is because we know that the Quality of Life Strategy is actually addressing the source (or at least a significant part of the source) of the seeming repugnance.

It is worth noting that this is also important in light of an objection that is sometimes made against defenders of the Quality of Life Strategy. According to this objection, defenders of the Quality of Life Strategy are guilty of focusing solely on the nature of population Z, though the Repugnant Conclusion really asks us to *compare* Z with A. As it is sometimes put:

> [Tännsjö] does not really address what is repugnant about the repugnant conclusion. What is repugnant is the combination of two features; people's lives in the larger population are barely worth living, and people's lives in the smaller population are much better. Tännsjö only addresses the former...[26]
>
> Tännsjö, 2004: 227

The argument that I have presented above should go some way to responding to these criticisms. Whilst it would certainly be a mistake not to be sensitive to the comparative nature of the Repugnant Conclusion, it is not a shortcoming of the Quality of Life Strategy that it focuses on the comparison of a high quality low population world *to Z* in particular. This focus is appropriate. It is appropriate because, as argued above, what is (seemingly) repugnant is the superiority *of Z-like lives* over A-like lives and not merely the existence of a trade-off. (I shall return to this point in the following section in discussing Ryberg and Tännsjö's views on what life at A might be like).

3.5 The value of ordinary life

Consider a second objection to the Quality of Life Strategy.

> Ordinary privileged lives are much better than marginally good. This is shown by the fact that we could remove many good things from them, yet those lives would still be good. It follows that marginally good lives are worse than defenders of the Quality of Life Strategy claim. So the Quality of Life Strategy fails.

This objection has been raised by, for example, Nils Holtug:

> It seems to me that my life could be significantly worse than it actually is and be worth living.
>
> Holtug, 2004: 154[27]

It is worth setting the objection out clearly.

1. We could significantly worsen an ordinary privileged life, yet it would still be good.
2. If we could significantly worsen an ordinary privileged life yet it would still be good, then an ordinary privileged life is significantly better than marginally good.
3. (1, 2) An ordinary privileged life is significantly better than marginally good.
4. If an ordinary privileged life is significantly better than marginally good, then a marginally good life is significantly worse than an ordinary privileged life.
5. The Quality of Life Strategy succeeds only if a marginally good life is not significantly worse than an ordinary privileged life.
6. (3–5) The Quality of Life Strategy fails.

How should defenders of the Quality of Life Strategy respond? The obvious strategy is to deny premise 1:

1. We could significantly worsen an ordinary privileged life, yet it would still be good.

They should claim that if we significantly worsened an ordinary life, it *wouldn't* be good. This is in fact the strategy that they take. But a large part of their effort is actually directed at explaining why their opponents, like Holtug, think otherwise (and why they're wrong). To this end, defenders of the Quality of Life Strategy can – and do – appeal to a number of different arguments.

The basic material for one such argument has already been offered. It concerns the use of the expression 'a life worth living'. Note that this is the expression used by Holtug in the above quotation: Holtug's claim is that his life could still be significantly worse yet still be *worth living*. Defenders of the Quality of Life Strategy could argue that this is significant. Holtug may be right that his life could still be significantly worse yet still be *worth living*, but, defenders of the Quality of Life Strategy can argue, this doesn't entail that Holtug's life could be significantly worse, yet still be worth living *in terms of its welfare*. This is because, as we have already seen, defenders of the Quality of Life Strategy – following Dasgupta and Wolf – can, do and should reject the identification of a life of marginally positive welfare with a life that is barely worth living. The former is likely to pick out a much better life, all things considered, than the former.

In addition to this, defenders of the Quality of Life Strategy – in particular Tännsjö and Ryberg – offer additional arguments for thinking that Holtug and others are wrong to think that their lives could be significantly worse yet still worth living. I present two below.

The argument from loss of goods

Holtug's claim is that his life could be considerably worse, yet still worth living. Consider an example of how this might come about. Suppose that someone were to lose a limb. It seems like a case in which one's life would be significantly worsened yet could still be perfectly well worth living. Perhaps this is the kind of case that Holtug – or others who think similarly – have in mind. If it is, Tännsjö argues in defence of the Quality of Life Strategy, Holtug and others are seriously mistaken about how losses that they incur are likely to affect their welfare. Tännsjö's claim is not – as one might expect given his pessimism as illustrated earlier – that losing a limb would render one's life not worth living. It is rather that losing a limb would not significantly decrease one's welfare at all. Why? In an interesting passage, he writes:

> [H]aving often been involved in discussion with members of the disabled people's organisations, I have sometimes asked people with acquired... disabilities how they assess the quality of their lives, before and after the accident and I have *always* received the same answer... Once I had adapted to the new situation my life turned out to be no worse than it was before I acquired my disability. I have a different life now, but not a worse life.
>
> Tännsjö, 2004: 226

Tännsjö's thought, then, is that the loss of a limb isn't really a life-worsening loss. It doesn't dramatically affect quality of life at all. This helps in response to Holtug. It does so because, to the extent that Holtug's claim his life could be significantly worse yet still worth living is based on consideration of this kind of imagined loss (loss of a limb) it isn't really a case in which one's life has become significantly worse at all. The point isn't restricted to loss of limbs. It is a much more general point. The point is that changes that, from our present perspective may appear to significantly worsen our welfare, do not obviously do so given the way in which we adapt.[28] This more general point is nicely expressed by Ryberg:

> Conditions may strike us as worse than they would be because we fail to count in the fact that our preference might change with the new conditions... [T]his provides a further reason as to why a normal privileged life may be overvalued: it makes it seem much more likely that we would be worse off if something happened to us – e.g. if we got a handicap or for some reason were forced to live a less prosperous life.
>
> Ryberg, 2004: 247

The basic view that Ryberg and Tännsjö argue for here is supported largely by anecdotal evidence. But it can also be supported by more systematic studies.[29] This is a powerful argument. It shows that the kinds of case that Holtug and others may be imagining do not in fact support their view. They do not support:

1. We could significantly worsen an ordinary privileged life, yet it would still be good.

They do not support it because they are not cases in which one's life is significantly worsened at all.

Of course, one might argue that this is not sufficient. Aren't there some losses that one can incur that *do* significantly worsen quality of life? The answer must be 'yes'. But this doesn't represent a real threat to Tännsjö or Ryberg. In the event that even a privileged person *really does* incur such losses, Tännsjö and Ryberg will claim, it really is up-for-grabs whether that life continues to be good. Consider for example material losses that leave one unable to meet one's needs. Tännsjö and Ryberg need not – nor should they – claim that such lives have not been significantly worsened. But they will now claim that such lives really may be bad. Their claim, after all, was only ever that privileged lives – lives in which, for example, needs are met – are positive.

The argument from over-rating

The second argument is that we systematically over-rate the quality of our own lives. This is a consequence of a range of closely related distorting psychological effects, including systematic bias in memory toward good events and away from bad. The phenomenon is appealed to by both Ryberg and Tännsjö, but it receives its most extended philosophical treatment in work by David Benatar; Benatar refers to the general phenomenon as *polyannaism*. Describing the phenomenon Benatar writes:

> Many people deny that their lives... are bad... In fact however there are good reasons to doubt that these self-assessments are reliable indicator of a life's quality. There are a number of well-known features of human psychology that can account for [this]... It is these... rather than the actual quality of a life that explain... the positive assessment.
>
> Benatar, 2006: 64

Benatar marshals an impressive array of psychological data in favour of this hypothesis. I shan't recount all of it here: over-rating is undeniably a well-established phenomenon. This furthers the basic case against Holtug and others who claim that their lives could be significantly worse, yet still of positive welfare. Perhaps this is in part a consequence of the fact that they have likely over-rated their quality of life.

A challenge: Optimism, pessimism and an upper limit to human welfare

I have presented several responses to Holtug. One of these responses – used by Tännsjö and Ryberg – was based on the following claim:

Over-Rating: We systematically over-rate the quality of our own lives.

We have seen that this is helpful in allowing a defender of the Quality of Life Strategy to respond to Holtug. We will now see that it is something of a double-edged sword: it actually gives rise to a *new* worry for these defenders of the Quality of Life Strategy. In the remainder of this section, I set out this new objection and explain how defenders of the Quality of Life Strategy can respond to it.

Suppose that Over-Rating is true. It follows that our lives are probably *worse* than we think. This is problematic for the Quality of Life Strategy. It is problematic because the basic move of the Quality of Life Strategy is, recall, to claim that if we have the correct conception of what life at Z is like, then we will no longer find it repugnant that Z is better than A. This is clear in the second of the key claims that I earlier identified as follows:

> *A Surprising Claim*: A life of marginally positive welfare is not unlike the kinds of lives lived by privileged people today.
>
> *Paradox Resolution*: When we recognise this, the Repugnant Conclusion no longer seems repugnant. Although it may still be counter-intuitive, it falls within the bounds of possibility such that – given that we already have powerful arguments for it – we should accept it.

The worry is that Over-Rating undermines Paradox Resolution. If, as Over-Rating tells us, our own lives are worse than we think, then finding out that life at Z is like our own lives won't make us think more positively about lots of Z-like lives. So it won't make the Repugnant Conclusion any less counter-intuitive. We can represent it as follows:

1. The Quality of Life Strategy works only if life at Z is better than we thought.
2. If Over-Rating is true, then (even if life at Z is like an ordinary privileged life), it isn't better than we thought.
3. (1, 2) The Quality of Life Strategy doesn't work.

How should a defender of the Quality of Life Strategy respond? One response would be to double-down on the importance of Over-Rating. Perhaps we over-rate our lives to such an extent that even ordinary privileged lives are lives of negative welfare. Perhaps only the very best lives are of positive welfare. This would allow a defender of the Quality of Life Strategy to reject premise 2 of the above argument. It is, however, problematic. Firstly, many opponents of the Quality of Life Strategy – including, as we have seen, Holtug – will find that even the claim that ordinary lives are only marginally positive in terms of their welfare level stretches credulity. To claim that only the very best lives meet this threshold will be even harder to defend. Secondly, it is not at all obvious that the empirical data on Over-Rating would support such a strong claim: the case for it would need to be made. Thirdly, as we shall see in Chapter 4, the higher that we set the bar for a minimally good quality of life, the greater the problem that defenders of the Quality of Life Strategy face from a further troubling objection: the Reverse Repugnant Conclusion.

Given these worries, perhaps a better response is simply to place less emphasis on Over-Rating in one's defence of the Quality of Life Strategy. Note that it doesn't appear *at all* in Dasgupta or Wolf's presentation. Their presentation is, as I noted earlier, rather more *positive* in its emphasis; it is that life at Z is much *better* than we at first thought. This is, I think, probably the best way to go. But there is still an interesting move that Tännsjö and Ryberg can – and do – make: a move that may allow them to hold on Over-Rating. It is to claim that human welfare has a rather low *upper-limit*. I explain below.

The claim that human welfare has a rather low *upper-limit* is particularly central to Tännsjö's presentation of the Quality of Life Strategy. As I noted above, in initially presenting his view Tännsjö approvingly quotes Mackie:

> According to Mackie … 'a level that is really marginally better than non-existence must already constitute a high degree of flourishing, *and beyond this little further improvement is possible.*' (italics mine).
>
> Tännsjö 2004: 223

Suppose that this is true. It has obvious ramifications for how we interpret the Repugnant Conclusion. It entails that life at A in the Repugnant Conclusion – at least if we understand this as a population of human lives – is not as good as we might have thought. More specifically:

> *Upper-Limit*: The best human life – and so life at A in the Repugnant Conclusion – is only marginally better than an ordinary privileged life.

Suppose that this is right. It could potentially be used to respond to the challenge just presented to the Quality of Life Strategy above.[30] If Upper-Limit is true, then the best life – life at A – is much worse than we at first thought. This decreases the intuitive difference in quality between life at Z and life at A, respectively. Perhaps this could *offset* the pessimistic picture of life at Z that Over-Rating implies. So it is not repugnant that Z is better than A even if Over-Rating is true. The following diagram helps to illustrate (Figure 3.3):

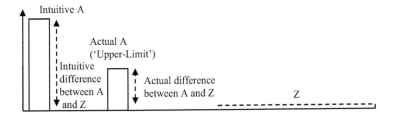

Figure 3.3

This diagram represents the comparison between A and Z in the Repugnant Conclusion. Life at Z is like an ordinary privileged life. 'Intuitive A' represents the excellent quality of life that we might intuitively imagine the very best lives to consist in. 'Actual A' by contrast represents the *actual* quality of life at A given the truth of Upper-Limit. The quality at Actual A is clearly much lower than the Quality at Intuitive A. The idea is that by realising that Actual A is true, we make the Repugnant Conclusion *even less* repugnant. We do so because we significantly lessen the difference between life at Z and life at A. And given this, the fact that even a privileged life isn't as great as all that – as shown by Over-Rating – doesn't fatally undermine the Quality of Life Strategy after all.

Does this help? I am not sure that it does, or at least not to a significant degree. There are several reasons for this. Firstly, suppose that Upper-Limit is true of *ordinary human* life.[31] There may be non-ordinary, or non-human lives of which it is not true. Suppose, for example, that future human life is artificially modified. These future humans are capable of living lives that far outstrip our own in terms of their quality (far above 'Actual A' on the above diagram). We can now reimagine the Repugnant Conclusion in terms of *these* lives. Wouldn't a small number of these lives clearly be better than an enormous number of lives that are like present-day privileged lives? And doesn't this show that Upper-Limit doesn't really solve the problem?

In responding to an objection of this kind raised by Gustaf Arrhenius, Tännsjö appeals again – as we have seen before – to the questionable nature of using intuitions about such unlikely cases in order to reject the theory. He writes:

> It is certainly a logical and nomological possibility that there could be some sort of beings capable of leading much better lives than the ones we live, but it is far from certain that these lives would be recognisably human…[I]t then becomes difficult for us to identify with them and once again our intuition falters.
>
> Tännsjö, 2004: 228

This is really another instance of the use of the principle that we identified above as the Realism Constraint:

> *Realism Constraint*: When assessing the Repugnant Conclusion, we should think about the nature and the quality of the lives of those who comprise the populations in familiar ways; our focus should be on recognisably human lives. These are the kinds of case on which our judgment is sufficiently robust.

I noted above that this is a generally sensible strategy, though it can be misused. It is misused if it is used to warrant ignoring genuine problem cases. One might suspect that its present use is a misuse in just this way: surely we can imagine future humans of the kind mentioned above.

Interestingly then Tännsjö fills out his use of this principle in defending his appeal to Mackie's characterisation of life at A.[32] He attempts to show how such lives (nomologically possible lives that are far better than our own) would be. One way of imagining what these kinds of lives would be like is simply to imagine creatures who enjoy, for each day of their lives, the kind of level of welfare that ordinary people enjoy on the very best day of their lives. This may sound straightforward. But, Tännsjö claims, such a creature is in fact rather difficult to imagine. The best days of our lives are characterised by, amongst other things, peculiar or unusual events, unexpected surprises, or achievements that are the culmination of long periods of effort. That is to say, they are precisely the kinds of thing that *couldn't* feasibly repeat day-after-day. We could, of course, falsify one's memory in order to produce the appearance of this kind of success from the first-person-perspective. But it is then unclear (at best) whether this person's life would still be a good one (as is familiar from 'experience machine' scenarios).

Tännsjö's point is somewhat compelling. Wonderful lives – of the kind that we might *think* ourselves to be imagining when we picture population A – are not like human lives. They are *very* different. The thought, then, is that this – in combination with the Realism Constraint, which effectively bars us from using far-fetched comparisons when evaluating the Repugnant Conclusion – is sufficient. Problem solved. I am unfortunately sceptical of this for three reasons. The first two are simple. Firstly, it relies on the truth of Upper-Limit. This is of course highly contestable and dependent on both philosophical theory and empirical evidence. Secondly, it relies on the Realism Constraint. I have already explained why, although generally sensible, I am wary of the possible abuse of this principle to illegitimately explain-away difficult cases.

The third reason is more involved. The basic worry is that the strategy being considered – using an Upper-Limit in conjunction with the Realism Constraint – misses the dialectical mark. The problem caused by Over-Rating is that it renders quality of life at Z *too low* to validate the basic claims of the Quality of Life Strategy. Upper-Limit won't fix this. It won't fix it because accepting Upper-Limit doesn't raise the quality of life at Z. Accepting Upper-Limit does something different: it lessens the difference between quality of life at Z and quality of life at A respectively. But that isn't the problem that we need fixed. This was made clear when discussing the 'trade-off' objection in 2.4 above. If the Quality of Life Strategy works it is primarily because what is repugnant about the Repugnant Conclusion is that we are trading off quality *to a Z-like life*, not that we are trading-off per se. So Upper-Limit fixes the wrong thing. So it misses the dialectical mark. For this reason, even if Upper-Limit is actually true of human life and even if it is acceptable to focus only on human life when assessing the Repugnant Conclusion, I still don't think it is the best response for a defender of the Quality of Life Strategy. A better response is to put less emphasis on the argument from over-rating. The argument from over-rating – and more generally, the pessimism about even some privileged lives that we find in Tännsjö and Ryberg – is, I think, probably not the right way to go for defenders of the Quality of Life Strategy. A better way to go is, following Dasgupta and Wolf, to emphasise *how good* a genuinely positive quality of life is. That is a more effective way to make the core point of the Quality of Life Strategy, though of course it now becomes less easy to defend this view against the kind of worry that we saw Holtug press above: we can't now appeal to the argument from over-rating to respond to him. There is, then, the beginnings of a dilemma for a defender of the Quality of Life Strategy.

3.6 Conclusion

The Quality of Life Strategy has been outlined and motivated. Clearly, it faces some outstanding issues. One concerns the use of the Realism Constraint to explain-away troubling cases. Another concerns the correct reading of the strategy – whether to take a pessimistic view of the quality of even ordinary privileged lives, and whether to appeal to Upper-Limit. More generally, there is a huge amount of material on quality of life that I have been unable to engage with fully here. I hope to have done enough to lay out the broad contours, as well as some of the key philosophical issues that arise from them. My real focus is on the more troubling philosophical issues faced by the Quality of Life Strategy. I turn to these in the next chapter.

Notes

1 For further arguments that can be used in conjunction with the Quality of Life Strategy as part of a debunking response, see Huemer (2008). This label is taken from Cowie (2017).
2 Dasgupta's work on population axiology includes Dasgupta (1969, 1991, 1995, 2001). The qualifications below are taken from his 2001: Part V, and 2019: Chapter 9. Subsequent presentation focuses on primarily on Dasgupta (2019).
3 For critical discussion, see Ryberg (1998).
4 See e.g. Arrhenius and Tännsjö (2017).
5 Dasgupta (2019: 34).
6 This is a prominent theme in (especially) Dasgupta (1991).
7 For a study of this, see Maddison (2001).

8 See Wolf (2004).
9 Wolf (2004: 76).
10 Tännsjö (2002), reprinted as Tännsjö (2004). I refer to the 2004 reprint throughout.
11 An alternative variant on this is to show that for all we know the repugnant conclusion could be true. This epistemic variant is argued for in Cowie (2017).
12 'We' refers to the fortunate among us: 'By 'we' here I denote me who is writing this and you who read it, i.e. affluent Western people who do not need to worry about proper schooling for their children, old age or health care'. Tännsjö (2004: 224).
13 Ryberg (2004).
14 See e.g. Feldman (2004), Crisp (2006).
15 For discussion, see e.g. Dorsey (2015), Fletcher (2016: Ch. 7).
16 For good general discussion of desire-fulfilment views and objective-list views respectively, see e.g. Heathwood (2016) and Fletcher (2016a).
17 Parfit (1984, 389).
18 Ibid.
19 For interesting discussion, see Wolf (2010).
20 These cases are discussed at some length in Parfit (2016) and – in the context of defending the Repugnant Conclusion – by Huemer (2008).
21 This may be the case if a 'perfectionist' view of welfare (e.g. Hurka 1993, Fletcher 2016) were true according to which for one's life to go well is for it to exhibit the excellences distinctive of its kind. So understood, welfare comparisons for different kinds may be ill-conceived. If not, a defender of the Quality of Life Strategy may be forced to bite the bullet on this case, arguing that, although counter-intuitive, it is not repugnant to do so.
22 A good general source of objections is Petersen (2006).
23 This is also developed in Cowie (2017).
24 For a good summary, see Hirose (2015: Chapter 5).
25 Crisp (2003).
26 Tännsjö is quoting Nils Holtug.
27 Compare Roberts (2015: 22).
28 This needs to be carefully handled. Even if it is the case that, sometime after the loss of a limb, happiness levels return to pre-accident levels, it maybe nonetheless be the case that there is a significant 'transition cost': a cost in moving from the pre-accident level to the settled post-accident level. This is discussed in e.g. Barnes (2016, Ch. 5). I am grateful to Guy Fletcher for pressing this point.
29 For a good summary of sources, see Benatar (2006: 64–69).
30 It is questionable whether this is exactly how Tännsjö intends Upper Limit to be used. For an alternative rendering of the argument – and subsequent criticism – see Petersen (2006).
31 It should be noted that Tännsjö concedes that A-lives may be significantly better than Z-lives because the former may be much *longer*, but so understood he does not think it repugnant that a sufficient number of Z-lives is better. Compare Huemer (2008).
32 Tännsjö (2004: 228).

4 The Very Repugnant and Reverse Repugnant Conclusions

In the previous chapter, I sketched the Quality of Life Strategy and explained its appeal. In this chapter, I set out the two most pressing objections to it and try to develop a common strategy for responding to them and so for saving the Quality of Life Strategy. Unfortunately, I fail. As such, I take the argument of this chapter to tell fairly decisively against the Quality of Life Strategy. Nevertheless, I take it that my attempt to save the Quality of Life Strategy helps to make some progress in how we understand it and why we should not dismiss it lightly (even if, in the end, we should dismiss it).

4.1 The Very Repugnant Conclusion

In 'The Very Repugnant Conclusion' Gustaf Arrhenius develops an objection to Tännsjö's use of the Quality of Life Strategy.[1] The objection is based on showing that Tännsjö is committed to, but unable to avoid, the Very Repugnant Conclusion. According to the Very Repugnant Conclusion – as initially introduced in Chapter 1 – a population consisting of an enormous number of *very bad* lives can be better than a population consisting of a much smaller number of very good lives *provided that* the population of very bad lives is supplemented by a sufficiently enormous number of lives of marginally positive welfare. It is represented by the superiority of Z^* over A in the following diagram (Figure 4.1):

Clearly, Totalism entails the Very Repugnant Conclusion. It does so because provided that the number of lives of marginally positive welfare is sufficiently enormous, the combined total welfare of this population and the population of very bad lives (i.e. of Z^*) will still be larger than the total welfare of the population of very good lives (i.e. of A).

This undermines the effectiveness of the Quality of Life Strategy. Even if the Quality of Life Strategy succeeds in rendering the Repugnant Conclusion acceptable, it doesn't succeed in rendering the Very Repugnant Conclusion acceptable. This is because the Very Repugnant Conclusion

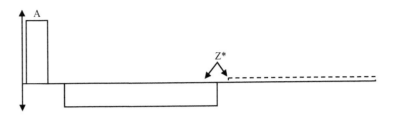

Figure 4.1

concerns bad lives: lives of *negative* welfare. The Quality of Life Strategy is silent on comparing populations that involve large numbers of *these* lives. As Arrhenius puts it:

> Even if we were to accept (I don't) Tännsjö's argument that the Repugnant Conclusion is acceptable because most people today have very low positive welfare, we are not forced to accept the Very Repugnant Conclusion. Since the latter conclusion also involves people with very negative welfare, Tännsjö's argument, which only concerns the axiological evaluation of lives with very low positive welfare, is not applicable.
>
> Arrhenius, 2003: 168

We can understand the argument is as follows:

1. If the Repugnant Conclusion is true, then the Very Repugnant Conclusion is true.
2. The Very Repugnant Conclusion isn't true.
3. (1, 2) The Repugnant Conclusion isn't true.
4. If the Repugnant Conclusion isn't true, then the Quality of Life Strategy doesn't work.
5. (3, 4) The Quality of Life Strategy doesn't work.

This is a powerful argument. How should a defender of the Quality of Life Strategy respond? The most direct response would simply be to bite the bullet on premise 2. This would amount to accepting the Very Repugnant Conclusion. This is problematic in two respects. Firstly, it is a very big bullet to bite. The Very Repugnant Conclusion really looks like it just *couldn't* be true. Secondly, if one does bite the bullet in this way, then the Quality of Life Strategy is effectively redundant in responding to the Repugnant

Conclusion. If one bites the bullet in accepting the *Very* Repugnant Conclusion, then surely one could accept the Repugnant Conclusion in the very same way (i.e. by biting the bullet). But if one did this, there would be no need to appeal to the Quality of Life Strategy at all.

Can we debunk the repugnance of the very repugnant conclusion?

Perhaps this is too quick. Mightn't it be possible to use a modified version of the Quality of Life Strategy to debunk the intuition that the Very Repugnant Conclusion is repugnant too? If so, 'biting the bullet' could be made palatable. This is roughly the approach that Tännsjö recommends. He recommends applying, and extending, the same basic method that he used in responding to the Repugnant Conclusion. His idea is that when thinking about the Very Repugnant Conclusion, we ought to focus our attention on what ordinary lives are like – in keeping with the *Realism Constraint*. When we do this, he thinks, the Very Repugnant Conclusion begins to look considerably *less* repugnant.

We can represent Tännsjö's basic strategy as follows:

> *Extended debunking strategy*: The Very Repugnant Conclusion is true (and so premise 2 of the above argument is false). We can support this claim, and explain away the intuition to the contrary, by focusing on what ordinary lives of negative welfare levels are like. When we do this, the Very Repugnant Conclusion no longer looks repugnant.

Tännsjö asks us to imagine a particular conception of what the lives in the Very Repugnant Conclusion are like. The very negative welfare lives in the Very Repugnant Conclusion are *long* lives in which each year is marginally negative. The very positive lives, by contrast, are equally long lives in which each year is marginally positive. So, for example, perhaps the negative welfare lives are lives of one hundred years, each of which is, annually, only marginally worse than an ordinary privileged life, whereas the marginally positive lives are lives of one hundred years each of which is, annually, an ordinary privileged life. Is it now repugnant (or 'very repugnant') that Z^* should be better than A? Tännsjö thinks not. His intuition can be further supported by noting that it may be that it would require a truly *enormous* number of marginally positive lives in Z^* to sufficiently outweigh the negative lives. Given this, and given that there are strong arguments for the truth of the Very Repugnant Conclusion, we should accept the Very Repugnant Conclusion.

Some examples can be used to help illustrate Tännsjö's point. Consider the following lives:

Ann: Ann enjoys a life that is about as good as a human life can be. It is long and largely free from ill-health. It contains many meaningful relationships and life-projects.

Zanna: Zanna leads an ordinary privileged life. She is well above the poverty-line and her life contains meaningful relationships and life-projects. Like anyone, however, she suffers from set-backs at work and in her relationships, and occasionally from ill-health. Annually, her net welfare is usually marginally positive but sometimes marginally negative.

Zelda: Zelda's life is very much like Zanna's except that the balance is marginally worse. As a result, annually, her net welfare is usually marginally negative but sometimes marginally positive.

We can imagine the Very Repugnant Conclusion in terms of these lives. Population A consists of Ann. Population Z* consists of Zelda and an enormous number of lives that are on a par with Zanna. Is it really repugnant that, so conceived, Z* is worse? Tännsjö invites us, plausibly, to think not.

This is an ingenious extension of the basic Quality of Life Strategy. It promises to make the Very Repugnant Conclusion itself acceptable (when combined with the strength of the arguments for it). Does it work? I don't think it does. While I think Tännsjö is right that there are some ways of describing the lives that figure in the Very Repugnant Conclusion on which it is *not* obviously repugnant that Z* is better than A, there are also some ways of describing the lives that figure in the Very Repugnant Conclusion on which it *is* obviously repugnant that Z* is better than A. This is all that is required. Consider, for example, the simple fact that there are some existing lives that are very bad not simply because of their length, but because of their day-to-day existence. There are, for example, those who live with severe mental illness, or chronic pain or both. These are ordinary lives. Many of us know people who lead these lives; they do not, therefore, violate the Realism Constraint. If the negative welfare lives in the Very Repugnant Conclusion are like *these*, then it surely is repugnant that Z* should be better than A. To see this, imagine that we add a new life to the above list:

Zorro: Zorro suffers from chronic pain and – hence – depression. As a result of his condition, he is unable to work and so is forced to live in poverty and debt. He has little or no family network to support him. His life continues in this fashion for many years. He dies from alcohol abuse in his sixties.

Now suppose we imagine Z* so that the negative-welfare lives described in it are like *Zorro's*. And suppose, furthermore, that there are a great many such lives. Surely now the repugnance re-emerges.

Tännsjö's core response to this kind of concern, as I understand it, is to appeal to a principle that he refers to as 'the principle of unrestricted instantiation'. According to this principle, it is only necessary show that there are *some* ways of instantiating the Very Repugnant Conclusion that are *not* repugnant in order to show that the Very Repugnant Conclusion is not repugnant *as such*. He writes:

> We should rely on the intuition that the Z[*] world is worse than the A world only if the intuition holds for whatever concrete instantiation of the conclusion we focus on. If we need a special instance of it in order to reach the conclusion that the A world is better than the Z world, then we are not dealing any more with the original argument from the repugnance of the [very] repugnant conclusion. Instead we are relying on some special aspects of the case that needs to be discussed separately.
>
> Tännsjö, ms.

The reasoning can usefully be understood by analogy. Suppose that someone were to claim that violent sports are bad. But suppose they were also to admit that rugby is a violent sport and that it is *not* bad. Clearly, this person could now no longer hold on to their initial claim that violent sports are bad. Provided that there are some violent sports that are not bad, it can't be the violence of some sports that is sufficing to make them bad. Much the same is true of the Very Repugnant Conclusion. Tännsjö thinks that there are some ways of instantiating its structure – as sketched above – that aren't repugnant. If he's right, it can't be the Very Repugnant Conclusion *per se* that is repugnant.

This seems correct but it isn't enough to get Tännsjö off the hook. Suppose, as Tännsjö thinks, that there are some ways of instantiating the structure of the Very Repugnant Conclusion that aren't repugnant. Still, there are some ways of instantiating just this structure that *are* repugnant. Provided that Tännsjö is committed to the claim that these aren't repugnant he is in trouble. And, I think, he is committed to just this. He is committed to it in virtue of his prior commitment to Totalist reasoning. Return again to the case sketched above. Suppose that Z* is comprised of a large number of Zorro-like lives and an enormous number of Zanna like lives. Tännsjö is still committed to the view that, provided there are enough Zanna-like lives, Z* is better than A, where A consists only of Ann. This is repugnant and its repugnance is not obviously mitigated by adding more Zanna-like lives.

For this reason, I don't think that the extended debunking strategy works. This doesn't mean that the Quality of Life Strategy doesn't work. It just means that it can at best work when applied to the Repugnant Conclusion. Something *more* is needed if defenders of the Quality of Life Strategy are to respond to the Very Repugnant Conclusion. Roughly speaking, they will need to identify a fault with the reasoning that leads from the Repugnant Conclusion – which they accept – to the Very Repugnant Conclusion. It is to this that I now turn.

Defenders of the Quality of Life Strategy should target premise 1 – not premise 2 – of the above argument. They should target:

1. If the Repugnant Conclusion is true, then the Very Repugnant Conclusion is true.

Defenders of the Quality of Life Strategy should qualify this premise. It is only *obviously* true, they should claim, for *some* derivations of the Repugnant Conclusion. More specifically, it is only obviously true for derivations that are based on Totalism. This isn't an objection to Arrhenius. He presents the argument against Tännsjö, who does defend a variety of Totalism. But it may allow some breathing space for *other* defenders of the Quality of Life Strategy: those who argue for the Repugnant Conclusion via something other than Totalism. For example, suppose that one rejected Totalism and instead derived the Repugnant Conclusion via the Continuum Argument. Would premise 1 then be true? This is something of an open question. Or suppose that one derived the Repugnant Conclusion on the basis of the Dominance-Addition Argument. Would premise 1 then be true? The answer to either of these questions could, in principle, be 'no'. This would allow a defender of the Quality of Life Strategy to deny that they are committed to the Very Repugnant Conclusion. I illustrate this below.

The Very Repugnant Conclusion and the Continuum Argument

Begin with the Continuum Argument, as sketched in Chapter 1. The Continuum Argument relies on the following principle:

> *Quantity*: For any populations, α and β, both of which consist of lives at positive, perfectly equal welfare-levels, if the welfare-level at β is only marginally lower than at α, then, if β has a sufficiently greater population than α, then, all else equal, β is better.

We cannot derive the Very Repugnant Conclusion from this principle. Quantity allows for comparisons between perfectly equal populations of very similar positive welfare levels and very different numbers of lives. It doesn't tell us *anything* about how to compare populations that are comprised of non-equal welfare levels, let alone populations that include lives with negative welfare levels. So it doesn't tell us anything about how to compare the different populations in the Very Repugnant Conclusion. So it doesn't entail the Very Repugnant Conclusion. So for derivations of the Repugnant Conclusion based on the Continuum Argument, premise 1 comes out as false.

But isn't this a bit of a cop-out? One might suspect that although Quantity doesn't *strictly* entail the Very Repugnant Conclusion, there must be some principle that underlies Quantity that *does* entail the Very Repugnant Conclusion. This is, basically, because one might suspect that the principle that really underlies the Continuum Reasoning is just Totalism. So although *strictly speaking* the Continuum Argument avoids the Very Repugnant Conclusion, this is at best a half-truth.

This objection is too fast. One can, without any underhandedness, assent to Quantity but not Totalism. There are two reasons for this. One is that there are genuine concerns with how to combine negative and positive welfare that might reasonably lead someone who assents to Quantity not to assent to Totalism. Totalism licenses simple sums of positive and negative welfare such that enough positive welfare can outweigh any amount of negative welfare. One may reasonably reject this (perhaps precisely because of the threat of results like the Very Repugnant Conclusion). The second reason is that unlike Quantity, Totalism simply ignores the significance of inequalities. One might quite reasonably think this mistaken. As such one might be unwilling to extend acceptance of Quantity to acceptance of Totalism. For these reasons, one could surely reject the claim that the Continuum Argument must rest on Totalism. Of course this leaves a question: what *does* it rest on? Is Quantity a basic principle? If not, what is the more basic principle on which it rests? I don't have an answer to that question. I return to it later.

The very repugnant conclusion and the dominance-addition argument

I have argued that the following premise is contestable:

1. If the Repugnant Conclusion is true, then the Very Repugnant Conclusion is true.

While this premise may hold for derivations based on Totalism it does not hold for derivations based on the Continuum Argument. Does it hold for derivations based on Dominance-Addition Reasoning? In presenting his case, Arrhenius claims that it does. He writes:

> One can replace avoidance of the Repugnant Conclusion with avoidance of the Very Repugnant Conclusion in a version of the [Dominance]-Addition Paradox.
>
> Arrhenius, 2003: 168

The derivation that we used in Chapter 1, recall is based on the following principles (in addition to some form of transitivity principle):

Dominance-Addition Principle: For any populations, α and β, if α consists of lives at a positive, equal welfare-level, and β consists of the same number of lives, but at a higher welfare-level, plus some other lives at any positive welfare level, then β is, all else equal, better.

Non-Anti-Egalitarianism: For any populations, α and β, consisting of positive-welfare lives, if β is more equal than α and contains both more total welfare and has a higher average welfare, then β is, all else equal, better.

Arrhenius's claim is not that *these* principles (Dominance-Addition Principle and Non-Anti-Egalitarianism) entail the Very Repugnant Conclusion. It is that variants on these principles entail the Very Repugnant Conclusion. In fact, his claim is that *weaker* variants of these, plus some additional, unobjectionable principles, will suffice. Specifically, his claim is that the falsity of the Very Repugnant Conclusion is inconsistent with the following four principles:[2]

The Egalitarian Dominance Condition: If population α is a perfectly equal population of the same size as population β, and everyone in α has higher welfare than everyone in β, then α is better than β other things being equal.

The Dominance Addition Condition: If population α and β are of the same size and everyone in α has lower welfare than everyone in β, then a population consisting of the β-lives and any number of lives with positive welfare is at least as good as α, other things being equal.

The General Non-Extreme Priority Condition: There is a number n of lives such that for any population χ, and any welfare level *A*, a population consisting of the χ-lives, n lives with very high welfare, and one life with welfare *A* is at least as good as a population consisting of the χ-lives, n lives with very low positive welfare, and one life with welfare slightly above *A*, other things being equal.

The Non-Elitism Condition: For any triplet of welfare levels *A*, *B* and *C*, *A* slightly higher than *B* and *B* higher than *C*, and for any one-life population α with welfare *A* there is a population γ with welfare *C* and a population β of the same size as α and γ combined, and with welfare *B*, such that for any population χ, β and χ combined is at least as good as α and γ and χ combined, other things being equal.[3]

I shall simply accept that it is possible to derive the Very Repugnant Conclusion from these four conditions: Arrhenius presents a formal proof and I am not aware of any terribly persuasive reasons to think that it or the assumptions on which it is based are mistaken.[4] The question is whether this poses a problem for the Quality of Life Strategy. It will do so only if the four principles sketched above really are suitably similar to those used in Dominance-Addition Reasoning such that someone who accepts Dominance-Addition Reasoning and uses the Quality of Life Strategy to respond to it should also accept those four principles. Let's see if they should.

We can begin by setting to one side the first of the four principles: the Egalitarian Dominance Condition. While this condition is not a part of the Dominance-Addition Argument offered in Chapter 1, it is surely undeniable. Consider the following diagram (Figure 4.2):

Egalitarian Dominance tells us that in comparisons between K and L, K is, all else equal, better. It is hard to see how could one possibly deny this. So I shall assume that all defenders of the Quality of Life Strategy would simply accept it even though it is rather different from the principles used in the Dominance Addition-Argument of Chapter 1.

This leaves three remaining principles: the Dominance-Addition Condition, Non-Elitism and the General Non-Extreme Priority Condition. Must someone who argues for the Repugnant Conclusion via the

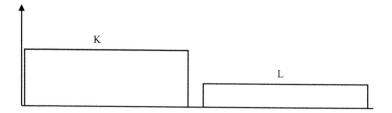

Figure 4.2

Dominance-Addition Argument accept these? It is hard to deny that they must accept both the Dominance-Addition Condition and Non-Elitism. This is because these principles are simply weaker, and hence more compelling, variants on the principles used in Dominance-Addition Argument. Begin with the Dominance-Addition Condition. There is, for our purposes, no significant difference between this and the Dominance-Addition Principle presented in Chapter 1. Non-Elitism is similar. It should be recognisable as a principle of the same spirit as Non-Anti-Egalitarianism. But in fact it is *much weaker*. The Non-Elitism Condition tells us that there is a population consisting of a sufficiently high number of people living at a sufficiently high welfare level, such that this population is at least as good as a population of the same size consisting of some less well-off people, and one person living a marginally better life than any of the aforementioned people. Consider the following diagram as an illustration (Figure 4.3):[5]

Both the Non-Anti-Egalitarian and the Non-Elitist will claim that in this kind of case L is at least as good as K.[6] The Non-Anti-Egalitarian will justify this claim by noting that L has higher total welfare, higher average welfare and greater equality than K. The Non-Elitist will justify it on much weaker, and so more compelling, grounds. Consider at least four respects in which the Non-Elitist justification is weaker, and so more compelling. Firstly, Non-Elitism only concerns cases in which the population of L is identical to that of K. The Non-Anti-Egalitarian view by contrast – at least as I have presented it – allows for comparisons between populations of very different sizes. This makes the Non-Anti-Egalitarian principle more contentious: one might be sceptical of whether simply increasing the population of L so that it is much larger than that of K is a genuine means of improving L over K.[7] Secondly, and relatedly, Non-Elitism refers to populations in which only *one person* in the inferior population has a superior welfare-level to anyone in the superior population. Non-Anti-Egalitarianism by contrast allows that, in principle, the inferior population could contain a *great many* lives at the highest welfare level. This feature of Non-Anti-Egalitarianism is a potential cause for concern: Non-Anti-Egalitarians must allow that a

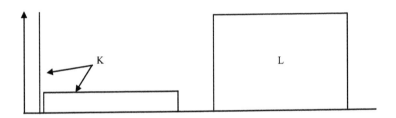

Figure 4.3

population that contains *very significant* number of highest quality lives may nonetheless be inferior. This will strike some as counter-intuitive. Non-Elitism avoids this. Thirdly, Non-Elitism specifies that the best life in the inferior world is *only marginally better* than the best quality of life in the superior world. Non-Anti-Egalitarianism by contrast allows – somewhat counter-intuitively – that the best life in the inferior world could in principle be significantly better than that in the superior world. Non-Elitism avoids this worry. Fourthly, Non-Elitism is formulated without reference to 'total welfare'. It therefore does not rely on the contestable assumption that welfare has a structure that allows for its summation across lives. Non-Anti-Egalitarianism by contrast *does* rely on that contestable assumption.

It seems, then, that someone who argues for the Repugnant Conclusion via Dominance-Addition Reasoning is straightforwardly committed to all of the first three principles in Arrenhius's proof: the Egalitarian Dominance Condition, the Dominance Addition Condition, and Non-Elitism. The first is uncontroversial. The second and third are simply weakenings of the principles used in the Dominance-Addition Argument of Chapter 2. That leaves only one principle if the Very Repugnant Conclusion is to be avoided: the General Non-Extreme Priority Condition. This is where defenders of the Quality of Life Strategy must make their stand. Can they do so? They may begin with a degree of optimism. Unlike the Dominance-Addition Condition and Non-Elitism, this condition is not used in the Dominance-Addition Argument of Chapter 2. It is a *different kind* of principle. It states, roughly, that a population of great lives is better than a population of marginally positive lives *even if* both populations are supplemented by one additional life – positive or negative – where that life is marginally better in the world of marginally positive lives than in the world of great lives. Consider the following diagram as a rough illustration (Figure 4.4):

In this diagram, with suitable provisos in place, the General Non-Extreme Priority Condition justifies the superiority of J over H: it justifies

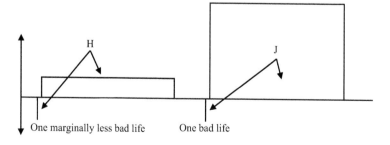

Figure 4.4

the superiority of populations with bad lives (really, a bad life) over populations with less bad lives, provided that the rest of the population (i.e. the large block in J) is sufficiently superior. If we are to be able to derive the Very Repugnant Conclusion, we must be able to make this kind of move. This is because the Very Repugnant Conclusion (favourably) compares populations with good lives to populations that have bad lives: a comparison that, as we have seen, Dominance Addition Condition, Non-Elitism and Egalitarian Dominance alone will not allow.

This is important. It means that someone who derives the Repugnant Conclusion via Dominance-Addition Reasoning and defends it via the Quality of Life Strategy isn't *thereby* committed to the Very Repugnant Conclusion. One could accept the Repugnant Conclusion on account of Dominance-Addition Reasoning but *deny* the Very Repugnant Conclusion. One could thereby deny:

1. If the Repugnant Conclusion is true, then the Very Repugnant Conclusion is true.

This will be possible if (and only if) one rejects the General Non-Extreme Priority Condition. This is a conceptual possibility. It remains to be seen whether it is *sensible*. I return to this later.

Where this leaves us

The argument of this section has been complex. We have been considering whether the threat of the Very Repugnant Conclusion shows the Quality of Life Strategy to be ineffective. Certainly, it presents a prima facie threat. We have seen, however, that there are potential ways out. While the threat of the Very Repugnant Conclusion does seem to be fatal for Totalists, it is less obvious that it is fatal for those who derive the Repugnant Conclusion via either Continuum Reasoning or Dominance-Addition Reasoning. More specifically, we have established:

> *Interim Conclusion (1)*: If the Quality of Life Strategy is to work, then it must avoid the threat of the Very Repugnant Conclusion. Derivations of the Repugnant Conclusion based on Totalist reasoning do not manage this. If the Quality of Life Strategy is to work, it applies only to derivations of the Repugnant Conclusion based on *either* (a) Continuum Reasoning or (b) Dominance-Addition Reasoning *and* the simultaneous falsity of the General Non-Extreme Priority Condition.

This is a conditional conclusion. It doesn't yet tell us whether the Quality of Life Strategy works. It only tells us what would need to be the case for it to work. I return in 4.3 to the substantive question of whether these conditions can be met. As we will see in the next section, there is a *further* conditional conclusion that a defender of the Quality of Life Strategy is also constrained by.

4.2 The Reverse Repugnant Conclusion

In this section, we consider a second worrying objection to the use of the Quality of Life Strategy. The objection was first presented by Tim Mulgan.[8] It appears to show that if the Quality of Life Strategy succeeds, it entails a result that is at least as implausible as the Repugnant Conclusion. So the Quality of Life Strategy fails. To see how this works, begin by noting that if Totalism is true, then it is possible to construct a 'reverse' version of the Repugnant Conclusion in which all lives are of negative welfare, and in which the large population is worse than the smaller but *more negative* welfare population. This is the Reverse Repugnant Conclusion. It is represented in the following diagram (Figure 4.5).

According to the Reverse Repugnant Conclusion, -Z is worse than -A. Why is this a problem for a defender of the Quality of Life Strategy? Presumably if the Repugnant Conclusion is true (i.e. if Z is better than A), then the Reverse Repugnant Conclusion must also be true (i.e. -Z must be worse than -A). The simplest way of understanding this is in terms of 'total welfare': just as A is better than Z in virtue of containing more total welfare, so -Z must be worse than -A in virtue of containing more total negative welfare. By itself this is not a problem: it is just another entailment of Totalism. But it becomes problematic if we apply the Quality of Life Strategy. According to the Quality of Life Strategy, life at Z is better than we might at first have thought: it is like an ordinary privileged life. Suppose this is true. It follows that life at -Z is also better than we might at first have thought: it is only marginally *worse* than an ordinary privileged life. This is a problem. It is a problem because the Reverse Repugnant Conclusion now

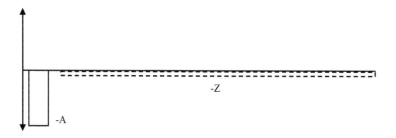

Figure 4.5

in effect states that a population in which an enormous number of people lead lives that are only marginally worse than an ordinary privileged life is *worse* than a population in which a small number of people lead truly terrible lives. And this is extremely implausible.

It is important to be clear on the structure of the objection, and in particular the role that the Quality of Life Strategy is playing in generating the troubling result. The Quality of Life Strategy raises the quality of life at Z relative to initial expectations. This has the side-effect of raising the quality of life at -Z relative to expectations. But the higher that quality of life at -Z is, the more implausible the Reverse Repugnant Conclusion becomes. Hence the problem. We can represent it as follows:

1. If the Quality of Life Strategy works, then the Repugnant Conclusion is true.
2. If the Repugnant Conclusion is true, then the Reverse Repugnant Conclusion is true.
3. (1, 2) If the Quality of Life Strategy works, then the Reverse Repugnant Conclusion is true.
4. If the Quality of Life Strategy works, then life at -Z is only marginally worse than an ordinary privileged life.
5. If life at -Z is only marginally worse than an ordinary privileged life, then the Reverse Repugnant Conclusion isn't true.
6. (4, 5) If the Quality of Life Strategy works, then the Reverse Repugnant Conclusion isn't true.
7. (3, 6) The Quality of Life Strategy doesn't work.

This is a powerful argument. How should a defender of the Quality of Life Strategy respond to it? There are a number of distinct strategies. Perhaps the obvious strategy for a defender of the Quality of Life Strategy is to challenge premise 4. It is to argue that the Reverse Repugnant Conclusion might be true after all. I shall begin by presenting – and rejecting – a response along these lines from John Broome. (I then switch my focus to premise 4.)

A Totalist response: vague boundaries

In *Weighing Lives* John Broome defends a version of Totalism against the challenges posed by the Repugnant Conclusion and the Reverse Repugnant Conclusion. The defence is based on a modified version of the Quality of Life Strategy. Broome's core claim is that predicates concerning quality of life are *vague*: as a result there are many lives for which it is vague whether that life is better or worse than neutral. Broome couples this with one of the canonical views of how to deal with vagueness: supervaluationism.[9]

This view of vagueness is based on the idea that there are many different possible 'sharpenings' of any vague predicate. A sharpening is a way of specifying the application conditions of a predicate so as to make its application precise. The key claim of supervaluationists is that we can permissibly assert that a vague predicate applies only when it applies on all of its possible sharpenings. Suppose we apply this to the neutral level. The result is that we can permissibly assert that a given life has a positive quality of life – even minimally so – only if it is positive on all possible sharpenings of the predicate 'positive quality of life'. This has the effect of pushing *up* the level at which we can assert that a life has a positive welfare, and so of what life at Z – given that it is a life of positive welfare – is like. It does so because there will be many lives that, although positive on some – perhaps many – sharpenings, are not positive on all sharpenings; there will be some very stringent sharpenings on which these lives aren't positive (i.e. on which they are neutral or negative). We will not be able to assert that these lives have positive welfare. We can represent it diagrammatically as follows (Figure 4.6):

This diagram illustrates how appeal to a vague zone (and supervaluationism) drives up the quality of life at Z: a population of marginally positive lives (i.e. lives at Z) is a population of lives that are positive *on all* sharpenings. That sets a high bar. So life at Z is better than we might have thought.

This is an attractive strategy. Although it doesn't use the same methodology as the Quality of Life Strategy presented by Dasgupta, Wolf, Tännsjö or Ryberg it has a very similar end-result. The result is that only lives that are really quite good by ordinary standards can be said to have (even minimally) positive welfare. The result is a lessening of the repugnance of the Repugnant Conclusion. Broome is aware that – much as for other defenders of the Quality of Life Strategy – this approach makes the Reverse Repugnant Conclusion a pressing issue. His response is in effect to use his supervaluationist rationale to deny premise four of the above argument: he uses it to show that the Quality of Life Strategy might be true even though life at Z is very much worse than an ordinary privileged life.

To see how this works, note that the very same reasoning Broome uses to push *up* our conception of what a positive welfare life (life at Z is like)

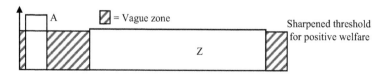

Figure 4.6

pushes *down* our conception of what a negative welfare life (life at -Z) is like. It does so because there will be many lives that, although negative on some – perhaps many – sharpenings, are not negative on *all* sharpenings; there will be some stringent sharpenings on which these lives aren't negative. We will then not be able to assert that these lives have negative welfare. The result is that we avoid the worst of the Reverse Repugnant Conclusion: pushing up the level for a marginally positive life won't require us to push down the level for a marginally negative life. We can push the former up and simultaneously push the latter down. We can represent it roughly as follows (Figure 4.7):

This diagram illustrates how appeal to a vague zone (and supervaluationism) both drives up the quality of life at Z and drives down the quality of life at -Z. So life at Z is better than we might have thought and -Z is worse. This is exactly what we want. It allows us to deny premise 4:

4.   If the Quality of Life Strategy works, then life at -Z is only marginally worse than an ordinary privileged life.

It does so because lives that are negative-welfare *on all sharpenings* will be far worse than privileged.

This is an ingenious response to the threat posed by the Reverse Repugnant Conclusion. It is however vulnerable to objection. Begin by noting that although in principle the various sharpenings *could* result in *both* a sufficiently high level for a minimally positive quality of life that the Repugnant Conclusion ceases to be repugnant *and* a sufficiently low level for a minimally negative quality of life that the Reverse Repugnant Conclusion is not repugnant, this *possibility* would need to actually be *established*. It could be, for example, that even the most extreme sharpening for 'negative quality of life' yields a quality of life that isn't bad enough by ordinary standards to make the Reverse Repugnant Conclusion acceptable.

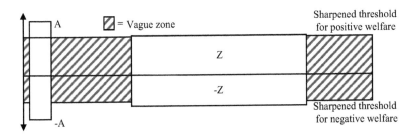

Figure 4.7

This is something that we would need to work out. We could not be sure in advance what the result would be.

Broome would likely object to this. He would object that I am illegitimately assuming that the thresholds for negative and positive quality of life respectively (on Broome's supervaluationist view) can be established *independently* from any assumptions about the truth of the Repugnant Conclusion and the Reverse Repugnant Conclusion. Broome denies this. He states quite explicitly that we should use the Repugnant Conclusion and the Reverse Repugnant Conclusion to *set* the thresholds for positive and negative quality of life respectively. He writes:

> The upper limit to its vagueness must be fairly high to prevent the positive repugnant conclusion form being repugnant. The lower limit must be fairly low to prevent the Reverse Repugnant Conclusion form being repugnant... These constraints are tight. We need to minimize it. I suggest this is the correct approach to determining the neutral level. The upper and lower boundaries of its vague borderline must be such as to leave us with the most credible consequences.
>
> Broome 2004: 264

As I noted in Chapter 3, this is a move that Clark Wolf is also attracted to. He suggested, recall, that we should understand marginally positive quality of life as a quality of life at which the Repugnant Conclusion ceases to be repugnant.

I think that this strategy is highly questionable. We shouldn't assume that both the Repugnant Conclusion and the Reverse Repugnant Conclusion are true and use this to set the limits for the vagueness of the predicates 'positive quality of life' and 'negative quality of life'. These should be established independently. They should be established independently because one or more of the Repugnant Conclusion and the Reverse Repugnant Conclusion *might be false*. This is surely up-for-grabs. We should not build the assumption of their truth into the specification of the sharpened boundaries of the predicates that we are using to help show that they could be true.

Let's set this aside however. Let's suppose that we can simply set the levels of positive and negative quality of life respectively at whatever points we would need to – assuming that there are such points – to make both the Repugnant Conclusion and the Reverse Repugnant Conclusion acceptable. A new problem now arises.[10] Broome needs the sharpened level for positive quality of life to be as high as possible in order to make the Repugnant Conclusion as acceptable as possible. And he also needs the level for negative quality of life as *low* as possible in order to make the Reverse Repugnant Conclusion seem as acceptable as possible. The result is now that there will be a very wide 'vague zone': a zone in which we can't say that the lives within it are either positive or negative. This wide vague zone is problematic. Consider the following diagram (Figure 4.8):

F and G represent populations with welfare levels that fall within the vague zone, but at either end: one *almost* positive, one *almost* negative. The broader the vague zone, the more different these lives are from one another. Yet on the supervaluationist reasoning that we are using, we couldn't say that F is better than G. This is deeply implausible. But it is a consequence of setting the thresholds for positive quality of life and negative quality of life respectively far apart in order to make both the Repugnant Conclusion and the Reverse Repugnant Conclusion acceptable. This is surely sufficient to warrant us in rejecting the Totalist response to the problem posed by the Reverse Repugnant Conclusion.[11]

I don't think, then, that rejecting premise 4 – at least in the way that Broome has suggested – is the best way for a defender of the Quality of Life Strategy to respond to the Reverse Repugnant Conclusion. A better response – the response that I develop below – concerns the second premise of the above argument:

2. If the Repugnant Conclusion is true, then the Reverse Repugnant Conclusion is true.

I shall argue that the status of this premise depends on how the Repugnant Conclusion is derived: whether from Totalism, Continuum Reasoning, or Dominance-Addition Reasoning. To this point (in this section), I have focused only on Totalism: I justified the entailment from the Repugnant Conclusion to the Reverse Repugnant Conclusion via the Totalism-based claim that if Z is better than A in virtue of containing more total welfare, then -Z must be worse than -A in virtue of containing more total negative welfare. It is not obvious however that this rationale transfers to justifications

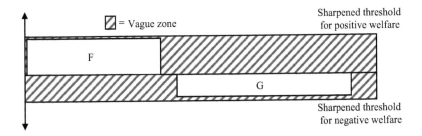

Figure 4.8

of the Repugnant Conclusion based on either Continuum Reasoning or Dominance-Addition Reasoning. So it is not obvious that premise 2 is true for these alternative derivations.

The Reverse Repugnant Conclusion and the Continuum Argument

We are concerned with premise 2:

2. If the Repugnant Conclusion is true, then the Reverse Repugnant Conclusion is true.

On *Totalist* derivations of the Repugnant Conclusion this premise is true. As we have seen, however, Totalism is not the only route to the Repugnant Conclusion. There are other routes. Do they also entail the Reverse Repugnant Conclusion? If not, a defender of the Quality of Life Strategy could have some breathing space.

Begin with the Continuum Argument. Suppose that one argues for the Repugnant Conclusion in this way. Would one thereby be committed to the Reverse Repugnant Conclusion? Strictly speaking, the answer is 'no'. The principle behind Continuum Reasoning as formulated in Chapter 1 – *Quantity* – tells us that, all else equal, for populations of perfectly equal positive welfare, small losses in quality of life can be compensated for by large gains in quantity of lives. This does not entail that for populations of perfectly equal *negative* welfare, small losses in quality of life can be compensated for by large gains in quantity of lives. So it does not entail the Reverse Repugnant Conclusion. So perhaps those who argue for the Repugnant Conclusion via Continuum Reasoning can reject premise 2.

Unfortunately, this is too quick. Although it is *strictly* true that Quantity doesn't entail the Reverse Repugnant Conclusion, this is a cheat. In reality it is hard to find a principled reason to stop Quantity generalising so as to entail the Reverse Repugnant Conclusion. All that we would need to show is that one who accepts Quantity should also accept the negative version of it – call it *Quantity (Negative)* – that deals entirely with lives of negative welfare. The former effectively states that small decreases in the welfare of positive lives can be outweighed in terms of total goodness by sufficiently large increases in population. The latter would state that small improvements in the welfare of negative lives can be outweighed in terms of total badness by sufficiently large increases in population. Both are below:

Quantity: For any populations, α and β, both of which consist of lives at positive, perfectly equal welfare-levels, if the welfare-level at β is only

marginally lower than at α, then, if β has a sufficiently greater population than α, then, all else equal, β is better.

Quantity (Negative): For any populations, α and β, both of which consist of lives at *negative*, perfectly equal welfare-levels, if the welfare-
level at β is only marginally less negative (i.e. more positive) than at
α, then, if β has a sufficiently greater population than α, then, all else
equal, β is worse.

It is hard to see why one would accept Quantity without accepting Quantity
(Negative). Note that – in case one wondered – this is quite consistent with
the claim of the previous section that someone who argues for the Repugnant
Conclusion via Continuum Reasoning could avoid the Very Repugnant
Conclusion. In order to entail the Very Repugnant Conclusion, Continuum
Reasoning would need to be significantly modified so as to apply to both
(a) a claim about the (comparative) goodness of populations that contain a
mix of positive and negative welfare lives and (b) *non-equal* populations.
These represent significant extensions that a defender of Quantity could
feasibly, and in principled fashion deny. By contrast, it is difficult to see
how Continuum Reasoning would not generalise to perfectly equal, and
entirely negative populations. And if it does, then it entails the Reverse
Repugnant Conclusion. So those who argue for the Repugnant Conclusion
via Continuum Reasoning should accept premise 2 after all. So Mulgan's
objection has bite against those who argue for the Repugnant Conclusion
via Continuum Reasoning.

The reverse repugnant conclusion and the dominance-addition argument

We are considering the second premise of a troubling argument for defenders of the Quality of Life Strategy:

2. If the Repugnant Conclusion is true, then the Reverse Repugnant
   Conclusion is true.

Defenders of the Quality of Life Strategy should want to deny this premise. So far though the prospects look bleak. Both Totalism and Continuum-
based arguments for the Repugnant Conclusion seem to entail the Reverse
Repugnant Conclusion. That leaves one kind of argument for the Repugnant
Conclusion: the Dominance-Addition Argument. Is someone who argued for
the Repugnant Conclusion in this way committed to the Reverse Repugnant
Conclusion? Basically, I think the answer is 'not obviously'. This is great
news for defenders of the Quality of Life Strategy. It gives them breathing
space in responding to Mulgan's objection.

Recall the basic principles behind Dominance-Addition Reasoning from Chapter 2 (I shall simply work with these (for ease) rather than with weaker versions, and shall assume Transitivity):

> *Dominance-Addition Principle*: For any populations, α and β, if α consists of lives at a positive, equal welfare-level, and β consists of the same number of lives, but at a higher welfare-level, plus some other lives at any positive welfare level, then β is, all else equal, better.

> *Non-Anti-Egalitarianism*: For any populations, α and β, both of which consist of positive-welfare lives, if β is more equal than α and contains both more total welfare and has a higher average welfare, then β is, all else equal, better.

These yield the Repugnant Conclusion. Do these principles, or suitably trivial modifications of them also yield the Reverse Repugnant Conclusion? Consider the following diagram (Figure 4.9):

This is negative 'mirror image' of the (first stage of the) diagram used in presenting the Dominance-Addition Argument in Chapter 1. If premise 2 is to be true, the populations represented in these diagrams must get progressively *worse* as we move from left to right, just as in Dominance-Addition Reasoning they get *better* as we move from left to right. This requires the truth of principles that describe these transformations as being *worse-making*. The principles that could do this are:

> *Dominance-Addition Principle (Negative)*: For any populations, α and β, if α consists of lives at a negative, equal welfare-level, and β consists of the same number of lives, but at a more negative welfare-level, plus some other lives at any negative welfare level, then β is, all else equal, worse.

> *Non-Anti-Egalitarianism (Negative)*: For any populations, α and β, both of which consist of negative-welfare lives, if β is less equal than α and contains more total negative welfare and has a lower average welfare, then β is, all else equal, worse.

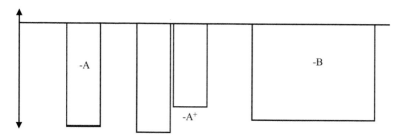

Figure 4.9

These principles describe the transformations as we move from A to -A⁺ and from -A⁺ to -B, and they describe those transformations as *worse-making*: they describe them in a way that would allow us to infer that -B is worse than -A. Is someone who is committed to their positive counterparts (i.e. the Dominance-Addition Principle and Non-Anti-Egalitarianism) committed to the truth of these negative versions? It is only if the answer is 'yes' that a Dominance-Addition Argument for the Repugnant Conclusion entails the Reverse Repugnant Conclusion.

I shall simply assume that one who is committed to Dominance Addition is committed to Dominance Addition (Negative). But Non-Anti-Egalitarianism is more complicated. I don't think that one who accepts Non-Anti-Egalitarianism is *obviously* thereby committed to Non-Anti-Egalitarianism (Negative). This is good news for a defender of The Quality of Life Strategy as it creates the space necessary to deny premise 2, and so respond to Mulgan.

Why doesn't Non-Anti-Egalitarianism obviously entail Non-Anti-Egalitarianism (Negative)? Take a step back. The original Non-Anti-Egalitarian principle is really concerned with populations that improve in *three respects*: total welfare, average welfare and level of equality.[12] It states that if a population is improved in all of these three respects, it is improved overall, or at least not worsened. This is what happens as we move from A⁺ to B in ordinary, positive Dominance-Addition Reasoning. The following table illustrates clearly (Table 4.1).

Presumably then, if Non-Anti-Egalitarianism is to entail Non-Anti-Egalitarianism (Negative), then the latter must concern three corresponding respects in which a population is *worsened*. A population must be worsened with respect to total welfare, average welfare and equality. Only then can we obviously infer from the truth of Non-Anti-Egalitarianism to the truth of its negative variant. This is where a defender of the Quality of Life Strategy can drive a wedge. Look again at the diagram (below) that illustrates the beginning of 'reverse' version of Dominance-Addition Reasoning. We can see clearly that in moving from -A⁺ to -B the population only worsens in *two* respects: total welfare and average welfare. In terms of equality, it actually gets *better*. The population *improves*. This is made explicit below (Figure 4.10):

Table 4.1

	Total Welfare	Average Welfare	Equality	Overall
From A⁺ to B	Improves	Improves	Improves	Improves

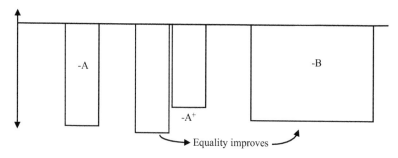

Figure 4.10

Table 4.2

	Total Welfare	*Average Welfare*	*Equality*	*Overall*
From A⁺ to B	Improves	Improves	Improves	Improves
From -A⁺ to -B	Worsens	Worsens	*Improves*	?

It is a consequence of this that we can't simply assume that someone who accepts Non-Anti-Egalitarianism must accept Non-Anti-Egalitarianism (Negative). There is no straightforward entailment from the former to the latter, as the following table makes clear (Table 4.2):

If there were to be a straightforward entailment form Non-Anti-Egalitarianism to Non-Anti-Egalitarianism (Negative) the italicised 'Improves' in the above diagram would need to read 'Worsens'.

We have won some breathing space for a defender of the Quality of Life Strategy. If one argues for the Repugnant Conclusion via Dominance-Addition Reasoning, then the following premise of Mulgan's argument is not *obviously* true:

2. If the Repugnant Conclusion is true, then the Reverse Repugnant Conclusion is true.

One might object as follows:

> Couldn't we just re-formulate Non-Anti-Egalitarianism (Negative) so as to concern populations that become more unequal? If so, then it would concern populations that become worse in three respects (not

just two). And so it would function in exactly the same way as Non-Anti-Egalitarianism. So one who accepts Non-Anti-Egalitarianism would be required to accept Non-Anti-Egalitarianism (Negative). So premise 2 would be true after all.

It is important to see why this objection misses the mark. It is important to understand why. Suppose that we did reformulate Non-Anti-Egalitarianism (Negative) in the suggested fashion (i.e. so as to concern populations made more *unequal*). This *would* describe a worse-making transformation in a population (or at least it would if Non-Anti-Egalitarianism describes a better-making transformation). But it would not save premise 2. The reason it wouldn't save premise 2 is that this modified version of Non-Anti-Egalitarianism (Negative) wouldn't allow us to deduce the Reverse Repugnant Conclusion. In order to deduce the Reverse Repugnant Conclusion, we need a principle that *both* makes the population more equal *and* simultaneously worsens it. This is because the Reverse Repugnant Conclusion concerns a population (-Z) that is *perfectly equal* in its welfare level. A principle for transforming populations that introduces *inequality* won't allow this. So while it may be true, it won't allow us to deduce the Reverse Repugnant Conclusion. So it won't save premise 1.

The Reverse Repugnant Conclusion and the Dominance-Addition Argument (2): equality and priority

I have argued that if we work with the Dominance-Addition Argument for the Repugnant Conclusion, the following is not *obviously* true:

2. If the Repugnant Conclusion is true, then the Reverse Repugnant Conclusion is true.

This is great news for defenders of the Quality of Life Strategy. Unfortunately, though it isn't good enough. There is a troubling objection to it. The objection was prefigured above. Perhaps the declines in total and average welfare that take place when we apply Non-Anti-Egalitarianism (Negative) to move from -A$^+$ to -B outweigh the gains that result from the improved equality. So the population is worsened in the move from -A+ to -B after all. So the Repugnant Conclusion does entail the Reverse Repugnant Conclusion. This is in fact very plausible. One reason that it is plausible is that there are well-known arguments – 'levelling down' arguments – for thinking that if equality is intrinsically valuable at all, it can be so only as one value among many, and that its value can be outweighed.[13] So if the Reverse Repugnant Conclusion is to be blocked, then, it must be because a very strong form of egalitarianism indeed is true: a version on which gains in equality trump potentially large losses in total and average welfare. This is surely implausible.

Does this mean that premise 2 is true after all, and so that the Quality of Life Strategy fails? There is one last line of defence for a defender of the Quality of Life Strategy. It concerns a *second* disanalogy between Non-Anti-Egalitarianism and Non-Anti-Egalitarianism (Negative) that we did not identify above – a disanalogy with respect to *the welfare of the least well-off*. To see this, focus again on the positive version of the Dominance-Addition Argument and on Non-Anti-Egalitarianism in particular. As I presented it above the population improves in three ways as we move from A^+ to B: total welfare, average welfare and equality. But, in fact, the population improves in *four* ways: total welfare, average welfare, equality and the welfare of the least well-off; the least well-off are better-off in B than in A^+. With reference to the last of these four conditions, I shall say that the population improves with respect to *priority*. The diagram below makes this clear (Figure 4.11):

In this diagram, we can see that in moving from A^+ to B, the population improves in terms of the welfare of the least well-off. Their lot gets better. This is important. The welfare of the least well-off is plausibly an important measure in the evaluation of populations.[14] Improving the lot of the least well-off is, all else equal, a way to improve the population. As such, it is plausible that there are really four significant respects in which the world improves when moving from A^+ to B. We can now also modify the table presented earlier. We add in a column for priority (Table 4.3):

This opens up a new disanalogy that could potentially undermine premise 2. To see why, note that as we move from $-A^+$ to $-B$ the welfare of the least well-off doesn't worsen: *it improves*. Again, this is made clear in the following diagram (Figure 4.12):

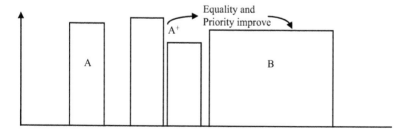

Figure 4.11

Table 4.3

	Total Welfare	Average Welfare	Equality	Priority	Overall
From A⁺ to B	Improves	Improves	Improves	Improves	Improves

Equality and
Priority improve

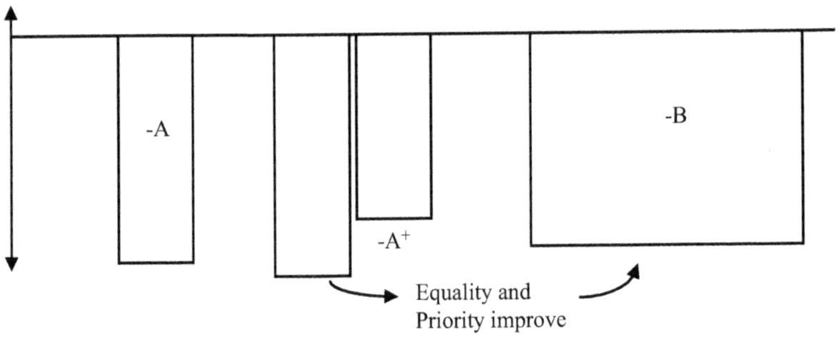

Figure 4.12

Table 4.4

	Total Welfare	Average Welfare	Equality	Priority	Overall
From A⁺ to B	Improves	Improves	Improves	Improves	Improves
From -A⁺ to -B	Worsens	Worsens	*Improves*	*Improves*	?

This is important. It significantly strengthens the case against premise 2. When we move from A⁺ to B, we improve the population in four respects. Non-Anti-Egalitarianism is plausible because by improving the population in these four respects, we surely improve it overall. But when we move from -A⁺ to –B, we don't worsen the population in these four respects. We worsen it in two respects (total welfare and average welfare) and improve it in two (equality and priority). This is represented in the following table (Table 4.4):

This strengthens the case against premise 2 made earlier. There are actually *two* respects in which the population *improves* as we move from -A⁺ to -B (equality and priority). So one really *could* accept Non-Anti-Egalitarianism but reject Non-Anti-Egalitarianism (Negative).[15] One could do so because the fact that something that improves in four respects improves overall doesn't entail that the fact that something worsens in two of those respects and improves in another worsens overall. One need only give sufficient weighting to the combined importance of equality and priority over total and average welfare. One could then reject premise 2 and save the Quality of Life Strategy (if only as applied to Dominance-Addition Arguments).

Where this leaves us

The argument of this section has been rather complex. As with the previous section, it has established a conditional conclusion. It tells us what would be needed if the Quality of Life Strategy is to work. What would be needed is for a Dominance-Addition Argument for the Repugnant Conclusion to be teamed with a sufficient weighting of equality and priority. Specifically:

> *Interim Conclusion (2)*: If the Quality of Life Strategy is to work, then it must avoid the threat from the Reverse Repugnant Conclusion. Derivations of the Repugnant Conclusion based on Totalist or Continuum-based reasoning do not manage this. If the Quality of Life Strategy is to work, then it applies only to derivations of the Repugnant Conclusion based on Dominance-Addition Reasoning, though only if teamed with a view that affords sufficient weight to both equality and priority.

In the next section, we assess whether this is sufficient to save the Quality of Life Strategy.

4.3 A solution?

In this chapter, we have considered two powerful objections to the Quality of Life Strategy. The first is based on the Very Repugnant Conclusion. The second is based on the Reverse Repugnant Conclusion. We have established a conditional response to each. We are now in a position to put these conditional responses together and assess whether the Quality of Life Strategy can be saved. The first conclusion was a consequence of attempting to avoid the Very Repugnant Conclusion:

> *Interim Conclusion (1)*: If the Quality of Life Strategy is to work, then it must avoid the threat of the Very Repugnant Conclusion. Derivations of the Repugnant Conclusion based on Totalist reasoning do not manage this. If the Quality of Life Strategy is to work, it applies only to derivations of the Repugnant Conclusion based on *either* (a) Continuum Reasoning or (b) Dominance-Addition Reasoning *and* the simultaneous falsity of the General Non-Extreme Priority Condition.

The second was a consequence of attempting to avoid the Reverse Repugnant Conclusion:

> *Interim Conclusion (2)*: If the Quality of Life Strategy is to work, then it must avoid the threat from the Reverse Repugnant Conclusion. Derivations of the Repugnant Conclusion based on Totalist or Continuum-based reasoning do not manage this. If the Quality of Life Strategy is to work, then it applies only to derivations of the Repugnant Conclusion based on Dominance-Addition Reasoning, though only if teamed with a view that affords sufficient weight to both equality and priority.

Putting these together, we now have clear conditions for the success or failure of the Quality of Life Strategy.

Both conclusions point fairly decisively to the failure of the Quality of Life Strategy to salvage Totalism-based derivations of the Repugnant Conclusion. If one reasons to the Repugnant Conclusion via Totalism and attempts to defend it via the Quality of Life Strategy, one will be vulnerable to both the Very Repugnant Conclusion and the Reverse Repugnant Conclusion. So the Quality of Life Strategy fails to salvage Totalism-based derivations of the Repugnant Conclusion.

Defenders of the Quality of Life Strategy would do better if they derived the Repugnant Conclusion from Continuum Reasoning. If one reasons to the Repugnant Conclusion via Continuum Reasoning and attempts to defend it via the Quality of Life Strategy, one will not be vulnerable to the Very Repugnant Conclusion. However, this approach will still fail. The problem comes from the Reverse Repugnant Conclusion. If one reasons to the Repugnant Conclusion via Continuum Reasoning and attempts to defend it via the Quality of Life Strategy, one will still be vulnerable to the Reverse Repugnant Conclusion objection. So the Quality of Life Strategy fails to salvage derivations of the Repugnant Conclusion based on Continuum-Reasoning.

This only leaves derivations based on Dominance-Addition Reasoning. If the Quality of Life Strategy is to have any chance of succeeding it must be used to defend derivations of the Repugnant Conclusion based on Dominance-Addition Reasoning. However, this is not straightforward either. Extra conditions must also be met. These are set out in the two interim conclusions above. In order to avoid the threat from the Very Repugnant Conclusion it would also be necessary for a defender of the Quality of Life Strategy to deny the General Non-Extreme Priority Condition. And in order to avoid the threat from Mulgan's Reverse Repugnant Conclusion, it would be necessary to defend a view that affords sufficient weight to equality and priority such that improvements in these can outweigh losses in both total and average welfare.

We are now in a position to properly assess the Quality of Life Strategy. Its success or failure turns, ultimately, on whether the defender of the Quality of Life Strategy can manage all of the following:

(i)   Argue via Dominance-Addition Reasoning.
(ii) Deny the General Non-Extreme Priority Condition.
(iii) Defend giving sufficient weighting to both equality and priority.

It is only if all of (i)-(iii) can be defended that the Quality of Life Strategy is off the hook. In the remainder of this section we assess whether this can be done. My conclusion is negative. It cannot be done. So the Quality of Life Strategy, despite its promise, fails.

Begin with condition (i). In a sense, this is true. *Of course* a defender of the Quality of Life Strategy can argue for the Repugnant Conclusion in this way. The question is simply whether the argument is sound! However, there are still some points worth making with respect to this. The first is that in the existing literature neither defences of, nor arguments against, the Quality of Life Strategy have been clear on the importance of articulating *how* the Repugnant Conclusion is being derived. In the literature, both defences of and arguments against the Quality of Life Strategy have not paid sufficient attention to the significance of *how* the Repugnant Conclusion has been derived. This is an important oversight. The second point worth making is that some defenders of the Quality of Life Strategy are actually attracted to Totalist Reasoning. For them, the conclusion of this book – whatever I argue with respect to conditions (ii) and (iii) – will not be welcome. So even if it does end up being possible to meet conditions (ii) and (iii), this will not have saved the Quality of Life Strategy in the sense that would satisfy many of its defenders.

Conditions (ii) and (iii) are trickier. Interestingly, although condition (ii) comes from the attempt to avoid the threat posed by the Very Repugnant Conclusion and condition (iii) comes from the attempt to avoid Mulgan's Reverse Repugnant Conclusion argument, *both* actually point *in the same direction*: some fairly strong form of prioritarianism. This is obvious with respect to condition (iii). The centrality of prioritarianism is also no less important with respect to condition (ii). Meeting condition (ii) recall requires us to deny the General Non-Extreme Priority Condition:

The General Non-Extreme Priority Condition: There is a number n of lives such that for any population X, and any welfare level A, a population consisting of the X-lives, n lives with very high welfare, and one life with welfare *A* is at least as good as a population consisting of the X lives, n lives with very low positive welfare, and one life with welfare slightly above *A*, other things being equal.

This condition basically states that a particular version of prioritarianism is false; it states that with respect to how good a population is, the welfare of the least well-off doesn't necessarily take priority over improvements resulting from the addition of a sufficiently large number of sufficiently well-off lives. This amounts to a denial of a strong form of prioritarianism. So both conditions (ii) and (iii) are pointing us in the same direction: the defender of the Quality of Life Strategy is being pushed toward a strong form of prioritarianism.

There are two major problems here. One is that such strong forms of prioritarianism are surely false: enormous gains in the welfare of all but one of the population can surely outweigh a tiny gain in the welfare of one. Suppose however that we set this to one side. Suppose we grant their truth. The second problem is much more compelling. It is that the truth of strong forms of prioritarianism are actually inconsistent with Dominance-Addition Reasoning itself. So conditions (i) and (iii) are inconsistent. Consider the following simple diagrammatic representation of Dominance-Addition Reasoning, as encountered earlier (Figure 4.13):

Focus on the first step in this diagram: the move from A to A⁺. Dominance-Addition Reasoning relies on the claim that this move constitutes an improvement. But if strong forms of prioritarianism are true, then it does not. This is because the least well-off are worse-off in A⁺ than in A. So conditions (i), (ii) and (iii) cannot simultaneously be met. So the Quality of Life Strategy *must* fail. The problem actually worsens if we factor in equality. Condition (iii) tells us that equality and priority *combined* are weighty. Suppose, then, that we factor in to our reasoning that losses in equality are worse-making. The result is that the move from A to

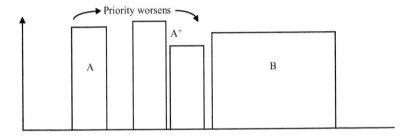

Figure 4.13

A^+ – Dominance-Addition – gets even less plausible: in moving from A to A^+, we worsen the population with respect to both equality *and* priority. So the case for thinking that conditions (i), (ii) and (iii) cannot simultaneously be met becomes undeniable.

We have, at this point, reached the end of the line for the Quality of Life Strategy. Its truth relies on defending a form of prioritarianism (and egalitarianism) that is independently implausible and the truth of which would undercut the reasoning needed to establish the Repugnant Conclusion in the first place. We can now represent the overall structure of the *master argument* of this book.

1. The Quality of Life Strategy works only if it avoids the objections from the Very Repugnant Conclusion and the Reverse Repugnant Conclusion.
2. The Quality of Life Strategy avoids the objections from the Very Repugnant Conclusion and the Reverse Repugnant Conclusion only if both:
    (a) It is based on Dominance-Addition Reasoning, and
    (b) Priority and equality have significant weight.
3. Conditions (a) and (b) cannot both be true.
4. (1–3) The Quality of Life Strategy doesn't work.

Despite its initial promise, and despite the fact that many objections to it have been too quick, the Quality of Life Strategy doesn't work. It doesn't work because, ultimately, the defensive moves that need to be made in order to rescue it from pressing objections cannot be squared with any plausible derivations of the very view that they are meant to defend.

4.4 Conclusion

The Quality of Life Strategy is at least somewhat effective in debunking the repugnance of the Repugnant Conclusion. But it runs in to closely-related problems. These problems come in the form of challenges from the Very Repugnant Conclusion and the Reverse Repugnant Conclusion. These challenges take the form of two troubling results that a defender of the Quality of Life Strategy is committed to, neither of which can be accepted. The best strategy is to argue that these results can be avoided: that they are not entailed by the Repugnant Conclusion on its most interesting derivations. I have attempted to develop this strategy on behalf of a defender of the Quality of Life Strategy. The roles of equality and priority in deriving the Repugnant Conclusion make this promising at first. In the end, however, it does not succeed. The Quality of Life Strategy cannot be rescued.

Notes

1 Arrhenius (2003).
2 I have used Arrhenius's formulation here except that I have followed the convention used to this point of using in Greek letters (e.g. α, β, χ) in formulating the principles, and that I have replaced Arrhenius's use of the set theoretic symbol for 'union' with the expression 'combined'. I follow Arrhenius's use of emboldened italicised letters to refer to welfare levels (I have not used any terminology to refer to welfare levels to this point).
3 For up-to-date renderings of this, see Arrhenius's (forthcoming) *Population Ethics* in which he presents a series of six 'impossibility theorems', developing on his 2009.
4 Perhaps the best candidate is a denial of assumptions about the ordering of welfare levels – 'simple steps' – that is also used in Quantity and that I have assumed to this point (and that defenders of the Quality of Life Strategy have no particular reason to deny). For some discussion, see Thomas (2017).
5 This diagram is used as an aid, but it should not be over-interpreted. It both represents total welfare, which is not referred to by the principle and fails to represent population χ (as referred to in Arrhenius's condition).
6 The Non-Anti-Egalitarian, as I have presented the view, will actually claim that L is *better*.
7 Perhaps because such an increase would render them incommensurable. See e.g. Temkin's (2012) 'spectrum arguments' and Chang (2016) for discussion. Temkin takes these cases to warrant qualified rejection of the transitivity of 'better than'. Chang, likewise, introduces a fourth value in addition to 'better than', worse than' and 'equally good': 'on a par'. However one could in principle allow that some populations are incommensurable in virtue of (for example) their very different sizes, without taking this to count against transitivity.
8 Mulgan 2002).
9 Broome (2004: Chapter 12).
10 Mulgan 2002: 364).
11 Broome acknowledges this problem in the passage quoted above but thinks that it simply represents a further constraint on the specification of the neutral level.
12 It is possible to run my arguments of this section by using weaker versions of the Non-Anti-Egalitarian Principle – versions that do not require welfare to be structured in such a way that we can make sense of reference to 'total welfare' or even 'average welfare'. But it is much easier to see the basic point if we think in this way – in terms of both the diagrams and tables referred to in this section – if we think in this way.
13 The classic presentation of the levelling-down argument is Parfit (1991). Note that I am not assuming that the levelling down argument shows that egalitarianism is false (nor should I: for defence of egalitarianism against this objection, see e.g. Temkin 1993). I am merely assuming that it shows that that any plausible form of egalitarianism must be a form of value pluralism.
14 Versions of prioritarianism are defended by e.g. Rawls (1971) and Parfit (1991). For discussion see Hirose 2015: Chapter 4).

15 There is a question-mark as regards whether prioritarian reasoning should really be applied to cases in which the less well-off people would not exist in one of the two scenarios being compared. If it cannot be, then the appeal to prioritarianism will not help the defender of the Quality of Life Strategy. I shall set this aside for present purposes – my response is therefore maximally charitable to the defender of the Quality of Life Strategy. I offer a different reason in the next section as to why the appeal to prioritarianism will not save the Quality of Life Strategy.

5   Conclusion

We are used to evaluating populations that differ in both the number of lives within them and the distribution of welfare amongst those lives. We say, as we look at projections of population growth for this century, that some possible populations are too big (or too small), that some are better or worse than others, that birth rates are too fast or too slow. What are the principles that allow us to make these evaluations? Some of the most plausible candidates lead to a highly counter-intuitive result: the Repugnant Conclusion.

> Compared with the existence of many people who would all have some very high quality of life, there is some much larger number of people whose existence would be better, even though these people would all have lives that are barely worth living.

We are faced with a paradox. An argument based on seemingly true premises that establishes a strongly counter-intuitive conclusion. How should we respond?

One obvious response is to accept the conclusion of the paradoxical reasoning. In order to do this, however, we would need to provide some kind of *debunking* explanation: an explanation of why the conclusion of that reasoning seems so clearly false though in fact it is not. One of the most influential – and independently interesting – approaches to this is the Quality of Life Strategy. It is to claim that many lives are in fact *bad* and that even ordinary privileged lives are only marginally good. This is an interesting and important strategy. It has much to recommend it; much more than its detractors have allowed. I have attempted to articulate and defend it. I have failed. In the process of trying to defend the Quality of Life Strategy, I have developed a new and powerful reason for rejecting it; a reason that is, I think, more powerful than any reasons offered to-date. It is that responding to the most compelling objections to it requires meeting inconsistent conditions and is therefore impossible. Those conditions, as articulated at the end of Chapter 4, are required to navigate the Very Repugnant Conclusion and the Reverse Repugnant Conclusion.

Where does this leave us? There are a number of options. One is that the reasoning that leads us to the Repugnant Conclusion – and the Very Repugnant Conclusion and the Reverse Repugnant Conclusion – goes wrong somewhere. Perhaps, for example, the principle of transitivity of betterness on which it relies is false.[1] Another option is that these seemingly implausible results are in fact true, but that we have simply yet to find a sufficiently plausible debunking explanation of their seeming implausibility.[2] One might think that these exhaust the options. There is, however, a third, rather different, option. It is that the fault lies not in our reasoning, nor in our intuitions about the implausibility of certain evaluative judgments, but in the nature of the nature of goodness itself. That is to say, perhaps the correct response is *metaethical*.[3]

There is a tradition in metaethics of arguing for a view called the *moral error theory*. This is the view that moral concepts are 'faulty' concepts. They are faulty in that they cannot be instantiated (compare the concept of a round square). As a result, the judgments that we make using them are, of necessity, erroneous. Typically, those who argue for this view do so via rather abstract metaphysical considerations about the supposed incompatibility of facts about goodness, rightness and so on with contemporary 'scientific' pictures of what the world is like.[4] Perhaps, however, considerations of the Repugnant Conclusion – and related paradoxes in the study of population – push us in this direction too. These paradoxes push us in the unenviable direction of accepting a set of mutually inconsistent propositions: a set that contains both the falsity of the Repugnant Conclusion, and the premises that entail its truth. We cannot do all of these. One conclusion would be that it is the concept of goodness itself that is faulty. It is a concept whose instantiation entails contradiction. If so we have a new argument from the paradoxes of population to the moral error theory, or perhaps more precisely to an evaluative error theory. Establishing this is a project for further work.[5]

Of course, none of this is of much use to those with practical concerns relating to population and welfare. The world population continues to grow while the 'carrying capacity; of the earth – as we deplete its resources – continues to decrease'.[6] We can, then, hardly avoid making and acting on evaluative judgments about the comparative goodness of population sizes. It is deeply worrying that the foundations of these judgments are so shaky. To some, it will no doubt seem intolerable. To those familiar with philosophical inquiry, it is unlikely to be surprising.

Notes

1 See especially Temkin (2012) and Chang (2016).
2 For example, Huemer (2008) offers some alternative debunking-style explanations.
3 This is a possibility that is touched on, though not developed at length by Arrhenius (2011).
4 For a summary of these arguments – and why they might fail – see Cowie (2019, Chapters 1–2).
5 Cowie (ms).
6 For more on estimating carrying capacity, see Dasgupta (2019).

Bibliography

Arrhenius, G. 2000. An Impossibility Theorem for Welfarist Axiologies. *Economics and Philosophy* 16: 247–266.

Arrhenius, G. 2003. The Very Repugnant Conclusion. In K. Segerberg and R. Sliwinski (eds.), *Logic, Law, Morality: Thirteen Essays in Practical Philosophy in Honour of Lennart Åqvist*. Uppsala Philosophical studies 51. Uppsala Department of Philosophy, Uppsala University. pp. 167–180.

Arrhenius, G. 2004. The Paradoxes of Future Generations and Normative Theory. In G. Arrhenius, K. Bykvist and T. Campbell (eds.), *Oxford Handbook of Population Ethics*. Oxford: Oxford University Press.

Arrhenius, G. 2005. Superiority in Value. *Philosophical Studies* 123(1): 97–114.

Arrhenius, G. 2009. Can the Person-Affecting Restriction Solve the Problems in Population Ethics? In M. Roberts and D. Wasserman (eds.), *Harming Future Persons: Ethics, Genetics and the Nonidentity Problem*. Dordrecht: Springer.

Arrhenius, G. 2011. The Impossibility of a Satisfactory Population Ethics. In H. Colonius and E. Dzhafarov (eds.), *Descriptive and Normative Approaches to Human Behavior: Advanced Series on Mathematical Psychology*. Singapore: World Scientific Publishing Company.

Arrhenius, G. 2016. Population-Ethics and Different-Number Based Imprecision. *Theoria* 82(2): 166–181.

Arrhenius, Forthcoming. *Population Ethics*. Oxford: Oxford University Press.

Arrhenius, G. and Rabinowicz, W. 2015. The Value of Existence. In I. Hirose and J. Olson (eds.), *Oxford Handbook of Value Theory*. Oxford: Oxford University Press.

Arrnheius, G. and Tännsjö, T. 2017. The Repugnant Conclusion. *Stanford Encyclopedia of Philosophy*. https://plato.stanford.edu/entries/repugnant-conclusion/

Barnes, E. 2016. *The Minority Body: A Theory of Disability*. Oxford: Oxford University Press.

Benatar, D. 2006. *Better Never to Have Been: On the Harm of Coming into Existence*. New York: Oxford University Press.

Blackorby, C., Bossert, W. and Donaldson, D. 2004. Critical-Level Population Principles and the Repugnant Conclusion. In J. Ryberg and T. Tännsjö (eds.), *The Repugnant Conclusion. Essays on Population Ethics*. Dordrecht: Kluwer Academic Publishers.

Broome, K. 2004. *Weighing Lives*. Oxford: Oxford University Press.

Chang, R. 2016. Parity, Imprecise Comparability and the Repugnant Conclusion. *Theoria* 82(2): 182–214.

Cowie, C. 2017. Does the Repugnant Conclusion Have Any Probative Force? *Philosophical Studies* 174(12): 3021–3039.

Cowie, C. 2019. *Morality and Epistemic Judgment: The Argument from Analogy*. Oxford: Oxford University Press.

Cowie, C. ms. Do the Paradoxes of Population Support Moral Error Theory?

Crisp, R. 2003. Equality, Priority, and Compassion. *Ethics* 113: 745–763.

Crisp, R. 2006. Hedonism Reconsidered. *Philosophy and Phenomenological Research* 73(3): 619–645.

Dasgupta, P. 1969. On the Concept of Optimum Population. *Review of Economic Studies* 36(3): 295–318.

Dasgupta, P. 1995. *An Inquiry into Well-Being and Destitution*. Oxford: Oxford University Press.

Dasgupta, P. 2001. *Human Well-Being and the Natural Environment*. Oxford: Oxford University Press.

Dasgupta, P. 2005. Regarding Optimum Population. *Journal of Political Philosophy* 13(4): 414–442.

Dasgupta, P. 2019. *Time and the Generations: Population Ethics for a Diminishing Planet*. New York: Columbia University Press.

Dorsey, D. 2015. The Significance of a Life's Shape. *Ethics* 125(2): 303–330.

Dougherty, T. 2014. Vague Value. *Philosophy and Phenomenological Research* 89(2): 352–372.

Ehrlich, P. 1968. *The Population Bomb*. New York: Buccaneer Books.

Feldman, F. 2004. *Pleasure and the Good Life: concerning the Nature, Varieties and Plausibility of Hedonism*. New York: Oxford University Press.

Finneron-Burns, E. 2017. What's Wrong with Human Extinction. *Canadian Journal of Philosophy* 47(23): 327–343.

Fletcher, G. 2016. *The Philosophy of Well-Being*. London: Routledge.

Fletcher, G. 2016a. Objective List Theories. In G. Fletcher (ed.), *The Routledge Handbook of Philosophy of Well-Being*. New York: Routledge.

Greaves, H. Forthcoming. Optimal Population Size. In G. Arrhenius, K. Bykvist and T. Campbell (eds.), *Oxford Handbook of Population Ethics*. Oxford University Press.

Greaves, H. and Lederman, H. 2018. Extended Preferences and Interpersonal Comparisons of Well-Being. *Philosophy and Phenomenological Research* 96(3): 636–667.

Heathwood, C. 2016. Desire-Fulfilment Theory. In G. Fletcher (ed.), *The Routledge Handbook of Philosophy of Well-Being*. New York: Routledge.

Hirose, I. 2015. *Egalitarianism*. London: Routledge.

Holtug, N. 2004. Person-Affecting Moralities. In J. Ryberg and T. Tännsjö (eds.), *The Repugnant Conclusion. Essays on Population Ethics*. Dordrecht: Kluwer Academic Publishers.

Holtug, N. 2010. *Persons, Interests and Justice*. Oxford: Oxford University Press.

Huemer, M. 2008. In Defence of Repugnance. *Mind* 117(468): 899–933.

Hurka, T. 1983. Value and Population Size. *Ethics*, 93: 496–507.

Hurka, T. 1993. *Perfectionism*. New York: Oxford University Press.

List, C. 2003. Are Interprsonal Comparisons of Utility Indeterminate? *Erkenntnis* 58(2): 229–260.

Maddison, A. 2001. *The World Economy: A Millennial Perspective*. Paris: OECD.

Mulgan, T. 2002. The Reverse Repugnant Conclusion. *Utilitas* 14(3): 360–364.

Ng, Y.K. 1989. What Should We Do about Future Generations? Impossibility of Parfit's Theory X. *Economics and Philosophy* 5: 135–253.

Parfit, D. 1984. *Reasons and Persons*. Oxford: Oxford University Press.

Parfit, D. 1991. Equality or Priority? *The Lindley Lecture*. University of Kansas.

Parfit, D. 2016. Can We Avoid the Repugnant Conclusion? *Theoria* 82: 110–127.

Petersen, T.S. 2006. On the Repugnance of the Repugnant Conclusion. *Theoria* 72(2): 126–137.

Rawls, J. 1971. *A Theory of Justice*. Boston: Harvard University Press.

Roberts, M. 2015. Population Ethics. In I. Hirose and J. Olson (eds.), *Oxford Handbook of Value Theory*. Oxford: Oxford University Press.

Ryberg, J. 1998. Generation-Relative Ethics – A Critical Note on Dasgupta. *Theoria*, 69(1): 23–33.

Ryberg, J. 2004. The Repugnant Conclusion and Worthwhile Living. In J. Ryberg and T. Tännsjö (eds.), *The Repugnant Conclusion. Essays on Population Ethics*. Dordrecht: Kluwer Academic Publishers.

Sainsbury, M. 2009. *Paradoxes, Second Edition*. Cambridge: Cambridge University Press.

Sider, T.R. 1991. Might Theory X Be a Theory of Diminishing Marginal Value? *Analysis*, 51: 265–271.

Thomas, T. 2017. Some Possibilities in Population Axiology. *Mind* 127(507): 807–832.

Tännsjö, T. 2002. Why We Ought to Accept the Repugnant Conclusion. *Utilitas* 14: 339–359.

Tännsjö, T. 2004. Why We Ought to Accept the Repugnant Conclusion. In J. Ryberg and T. Tännsjö (eds.), *The Repugnant Conclusion. Essays on Population Ethics*. Dordrecht: Kluwer Academic Publishers.

Temkin, L. 1987. Intransitivity and the Mere Addition Paradox. *Philosophy and Public Affairs* 16: 138–187.

Temkin, L. 1993. *Inequality*. New York: Oxford University Press.

Temkin, L. 2012. *Rethinking the Good*. New York: Oxford University Press.

Wolf, C. 2004. O Repugnance Where Is They Sting? In J. Ryberg and T. Tännsjö (eds.), *The Repugnant Conclusion. Essays on Population Ethics*. Dordrecht: Kluwer Academic Publishers.

Wolf, S. 2010. *Meaning in Life and Why it Matters*. Princeton: Princeton University Press.

Index

For Product Safety Concerns and Information please contact our EU representative GPSR@taylorandfrancis.com Taylor & Francis Verlag GmbH, Kaufingerstraße 24, 80331 München, Germany

Batch number: 08153772

Printed by Printforce, the Netherlands